Wrestlin

The History of I Wrestling

Tricia Andersen and
Diane Fannon-Langton

Wrestling Herstory: The History of Iowa High School Girls Wrestling

Copyright © 2020 Tricia Andersen

Edited by Diane Fannon-Langton

Cover design by Tricia Andersen

Top photo on cover: Megan Peavey wrestling a match. Photo by Brett McKamey

Middle photo on cover: The wrestlers who competed in Ogden at the first girls only division, January 2020. Photo provided by Troy Greder

Bottom photo on cover: Group photo at the second IWCOA Girls State Meet at Waverly-Shell Rock High School. January 2020. Photo provided by Tricia Andersen.

Dedication

This book is dedicated to every Iowa girl who represented her high school as she stepped on the mat. Your immense courage has paved the way for generations to come.

And especially to my girls, the ones who let me one of your "wrestling moms". The hugs and the talks have meant the world to me. Thank you for letting me part of your journey. So much love to each of you.

And to my own wrestler. You'll never know how proud I am of you. You and your brothers are the best things I've ever had a hand in making. I love all three of you more than you know.

Foreword

This was supposed to be Ali's book.

I was encouraged by a dear friend to write my daughter, Ali's, story. She is one of the very few girls to wrestle for both the east and west side of the state. She claims coaches on both sides of I-35 and my friend is one of them. This was supposed to be her book.

Except there were so many more girls before her who paved the way for her and all the girls she shares the mat with. Their story needs to be told first.

This book covers the major events that happened in girls high school wrestling in Iowa as recorded by the newspapers and news outlets of our state and across the country. But there are so many more stories out there. Next time you meet one of these athletes, ask them to tell you theirs. Some are good. Some aren't. All of them are heroic.

I am honored to share this history with you. And if I'm lucky, I'll get the chance to be their voice for years to come.

Tricia

This was supposed to be Tricia's book for Ali. Somehow she conned me into collaborating. What an honor to work with my very smart and talented daughter, who finds a myriad of ways to keep me learning.

Diane

Iowa's Early Girl Wrestlers

Iowa is known for wrestling just as much as it is for corn. One of the most renowned names in the sport, Dan Gable, coached for the Hawkeyes.

He began his wrestling career in high school in Waterloo where he won three state championships. He went on to Iowa State University to claim two national championships. After winning a gold medal at the 1971 world championships and the 1972 Olympics, he led the Hawkeyes to 15 NCAA Championships. Among those team titles, he coached 152 All-Americans, 45 national championships, 106 Big Ten Champion, and twelve Olympians. This included Tom and Terry Brands, who followed him at the helm of the University of Iowa wrestling program when he retired. Many national titles were won by collegiate teams in Iowa from the NCAA to the NAIA. As of 2020, the men's wrestling team at Grandview University in Des Moines won nine consecutive NAIA national titles. The only other college to do this is the University of Iowa.

Multiple Olympic medalists have come from Iowa including Gable, Ben Askren, and Nat Pendleton. Many more great Olympians, such as the Brands brothers and Cael Sanderson, were trained in Iowa.

Boys' high school wrestling started with intramural squads after World War I, according to a paper, "The History of High School Wrestling in Iowa," written by Loren Glenn Parker for his master's degree at Drake University in 1970.

Parker wrote, "The first high school dual meet was held Jan. 16, 1920, at Fort Dodge." The meet was between Fort Dodge and Mason City.

The first State meets were held in Ames and Iowa City in 1921, one on the west side of the state and one on the east. When the Iowa High School Athletic Association took over governance of wrestling in 1927, they consolidated the two state meets into one in Ames.

But what about the high school girls? When did they get their chance to hit the mat in Iowa? How did we go from the occasional female competing against the males to over five hundred facing off with each other in 2020?

While women were wrestling on the carnival circuit in the 1940s and the 1950s, the first mention of girls wrestling in Iowa high schools happened in 1971 at Van Buren High School in Keosauqua. According to the March 6, 1971. Ottumwa Courier, 32 girls committed to try wrestling, with more agreeing to come after the basketball season was over.

It all stemmed from varsity cheerleader Nancy Brown questioning coach Kerry Hinkle about why they couldn't have girls' wrestling on the way to the sectional tournament that year. Although Hinkle was met with a fair amount of criticism about girls wrestling with other girls, his turnout could fill two full competitive rosters.

The boys wrestling at Van Buren at the time couldn't do that.

Charles Bullard of the Des Moines Register added to the story eight days later by reporting the reaction the Van Buren boys had to the girls practicing the same sport. Calling the girls the "fairer sex", he mentioned that they had just spent the afternoon learning "the finer points to hem basting" before trying their hand at grappling. He also pointed out that they "were prettier and, according to their coach, Kerry Hinkle, faster and more enthusiastic."

The boys laughed at the girls at first, but once they realized how serious the girls were at wrestling, they supported them. Several boys volunteered to cheerlead for the girls while one of the more skilled guys worked with the coach to demonstrate the drills.

Coach Hinkle was very confident that a lower weight girl could compete with a guy her size and beat him. He said, "Give me three years with a freshman girl and put her up against a freshman or sophomore boy and she would rip him up."

The advantages that Hinkle found with female wrestlers was their ability to stay on weight as well as their quicker reflexes. Since girls didn't grow as much as boys in their teenage years, they were less likely to have to cut weight.

Nancy Brown, one of the girls that approached Coach Hinkle about wrestling, told the Des Moines Register, "In a few years I think a girl might try to go out for the boys wrestling team. But I think wrestling competition between girls teams might catch on faster."

Bullard described the girls in practice dressed in grey sweat suits ready to "do battle - in a ladylike manner." They began each match imitating the professional wrestlers known at the time as they looked for the moment to strike. One match Bullard described ended with a fake tap out from an arm lock while another was called when one wrestler's wig was torn off in a headlock. According to the website *goretro.com*, wigs were a popular fashion trend at the time.

NEW MAT LOOK. Girls wrestling has been introduced at Van Buren high school. Coaching the sport is Kerry Hinkle, show giving instruction to Nancy Brown.left. and Ruth Muntz. See Kitchens Klatter. Courier Sportsphoto by Bill Kitchen.

Bullard described the girls in practice dressed in grey sweat suits ready to "do battle - in a ladylike manner." They began each match imitating the professional wrestlers known at the time as they looked for the moment to strike. One match Bullard described ended with a fake tap out from an arm lock while another was called when one wrestler's wig was torn off in a headlock. According to the website *goretro.com*, wigs were a popular fashion trend at the time.

Coach Hinkle received little vocal opposition from the girls' parents but he suspected a drop in attendance had to do with parents telling the girls to stop. In interviews, the girls attributed being able to defend themselves as reason for joining the team. This prompted Hinkle to add judo, karate, and other martial arts to what he was teaching.

According to Bullard, when Hinkle told other coaches in the area about the girls who wrestled at Van Buren, he was met with "disbelieving laughs." His colleagues thought he was joking. At the time, the program was the only one that anyone was aware of in the United States, so competition was nonexistent.

However, Brown did believe that someday a girl would try out for the boys' team.

***

In October of the same year, the Altoona Herald noted that a girls' wrestling club began at Southeast Polk High School in Pleasant Hill, Ia. Forty girls came to the first meeting.

***

On December 6, 1973, the Spirit Lake Beacon did a brief story about Coach Ray Beal leading the girls physical education class in a lesson about wrestling. After commenting how easy it was to sink in the mat, a couple "handsome wrestlers" helped him show the girls a few holds. Those in the class then attempted the same thing. Although they enjoyed it, those in attendance believed girls would never wrestle for Southeast Polk.

While there was no mention made of a team forming, the Carroll Daily Times reported that, when surveying the seventh through twelfth grade students in the school district about new sports to be added to the activities budget, twenty-eight girls opted for wrestling. Even though it would cost them nearly $3000 to begin, in addition to purchasing a mat, it was the only one Carroll schools felt would receive an income back from spectators. However, the school district did not act on the surveys of the suggested sports which included girls' softball as well as girls' and boys' tennis.

Joining the Boys' Team

While the first girl to hit the mat against a boy happened in California in 1973, the same thing didn't happen until 1981 in Iowa. The first mention of girls competing in this state was reported by the Fort Madison Evening Democrat on February 8, 1981, when Caroline Lee and Julie Puffer petitioned to start a girls wrestling team at Central High School in Iowa City. They were allowed to explore if girls in their school wanted to start a wrestling team. Their high school careers were short-lived, however, when the Board of Education revoked their permission two weeks later. Phyllis Yager, the equity coordinator for the district at that time said, "Two girls are controllable. We were looking down the road where this could be a problem."

Lee and Puffer put in the training to be part of the team by running up and down the stairs at school as well as doing over a hundred pushups and sit-ups each day. They spent time learning wrestling on their own.

Despite the hard work the girls put in during the two weeks, they were met with opposition. Their male competitors cursed at them when they were paired against each other and told them that wrestling just wasn't a girls sport. Only a few in the crowd would cheer for them. The opposition to the girls performing on the team seemed strange to Coach Robert Stadlander, who said, "After thinking about it for a while, I guess it's that it isn't ladylike for girls to tumble around on the floor with boys. I can't see any big difference. They're in uniform and they go out there for the same purpose - to win."

However, in those two weeks, Puffer wrestled for Central against Washington High School in Washington, Iowa,

13

making her the first girl in Iowa to compete for a team. As reported in the December 18, 1980, Fairfield Ledger, she was anxious to compete but that "her opponent had a few qualms, too."

Puffer said, "Before the match my coach warned me that this guy looks real confident, like he's going to pin you in five seconds. I was scared. In fact, I was terrified. But I plan to do a lot more wrestling".

At first the boys from Washington wanted nothing to do with the match. Washington Coach Leonard Kull told the Ledger that he informed his team that "Central had some girls wrestling and that I wouldn't think any less of them if they didn't want to wrestle. None of them did".

However, when he found out that there was no one else for Central at 132 pounds, Mike Knelling didn't pass up time on the mat and faced off with her, pinning her in two minutes and 40 seconds. Puffer was disappointed in the loss. There was no opponent for Lee.

***

In 1986, Lisa Randall of Cardinal High School in Eldon. Iowa, was just another wrestler on the JV roster. The Ottumwa Courier reported on December 15 that she did well at the Albia junior varsity tournament the Saturday before, despite the fact that she lost.

"I really didn't want to come," she said, "but once I got here, I figured I might as well get it over with. I was afraid of losing. I didn't want to lose. At first I was nervous, but when I got out there, I wasn't. I kept thinking I'd get pinned in the first minute. I thought I'd do terrible."

She fell to Albia's Tony Nicoletto, 11-8. Nicoletto was reluctant to wrestle her and was glad that he won. Craig Reber, the sports reporter for The Courier, quoted Nicoletto as saying, "It wasn't that bad. I didn't want to; it was awkward. She's a girl you know. But I didn't really think about it out there. I didn't want to try anything weird. My coach just said, 'Beat her'. I was relieved I got it over with. I'm glad I beat her. I wouldn't want to wrestle her again. I just didn't like it. I don't really like girls wrestling. It doesn't seem right."

Cardinal coach George Loerzel praised Lisa Randall's work in the room, stating that she did every drill that her teammates did and, to the boys on the team, she was just another wrestler. He told The Courier, "She's expected to (do) everything everybody else does. Any drill we do, she does. She's learning and working hard. The other day she got a bloody nose in practice. She went and fixed it and came back and wrestled again."

GOING FOR IT!: Cardinal High School freshman wrestler Lisa Randall spins over the top of Albia's Tony Nicoletto as she tries to break him down during her first wrestling match Saturday morning in Albia. Randall lost a tightly contested match by an 11-8 score in the junior varsity tournament. Photo by Dan Nierling of the Ottumwa Courier.

Determination is seen in Randall's eyes as she takes the mat during a tournament in Eddyville. Photos by John Gaines of the Fairfield Ledger.

One of her teammates, Chris Terrell, also chimed in on Randall as a teammate. "I think it's OK. At first I didn't know how to take it. Now we treat her as one of the guys, just someone else to wrestle. She's pretty aggressive. She gets wins and she loses just like everyone else. It's not that different. People kind of think it's strange for a girl to be out but she's just someone else we have to wrestle."

A few of Randall's classmates also weighed in on Randall's spot on the team. June Davison, a cheerleader, told The Courier that it was great and that "there's a lot of varsity boys who treat her nice; they stick up for her but they treat her as an equal."

Davison's teammate, Rewa Price, added, "She's (Randall) not afraid to do it. At first I thought it was stupid, but she enthuses other girls to go out for sports they've never thought of. She's an example. And as soon as she wins, nobody's going to think of her as being different. They'll think of her as a wrestler.".

Lisa Randall was also profiled by the Fairfield Ledger on February 14, 1987. Larry Johnson, the reporter who covered the story, noted that Randall's locker was decorated for the upcoming meet just like the rest of the wrestlers on the team. Hers had a picture of the Cardinal mascot with its hand around the throat of their opponent's mascot, holding it off the ground.

Johnson followed it up with the fact that the Iowa High School Athletic Association didn't even track the number of girls who participated, citing that most only did so for notoriety. They seemed to do this to prevent there being a bigger issue of a girl on the mat than any other participant. Randall was one of a small percentage of females who participated in the sport. Most didn't last long before quitting.

"We get maybe four or five a year," Dave Harty from the IHSAA said. "Most don't last more than three to five days. Only a few — and very, very few — ever even want to try. So often, the case is that a girl is just looking for notoriety or publicity."

Harty also told the Ledger that, "We'd rather see them not compete; they do have other programs, but it's not worth wasting money in court over, either. To me, it's not feminine. I coached wrestling and I think that the moves and holds in wrestling are pertinent to a discussion of a girl participating in wrestling. But the Title IX Act of 1972 says that school districts can restrict girls from participating if there is a comparable program. And who has a girls wrestling team? Nobody has it. So if they persist, we just let 'em go. We don't treat them any different than we would a boy. But most of them find out that it's not for them."

Girl wrestler Lisa Randall of Eldon, in her room surrounded by pictures of her pro wrestling idols. Photos by John Gaines of the Fairfield Ledger.

As Johnson of the Fairfield Ledger stated, Randall was the exception to the norm described by Harty. She wasn't in it for the fame. In fact, she was tired of being interviewed. She had wrestled the entire season and had full intentions of continuing to be part of the team in the future. She said, "When I graduate from high school, I want to be a professional wrestler."

This was an obvious choice of career for her, according to Johnson. Her bedroom was covered with posters of professional wrestlers. A fan and frequent watcher of professional wrestling, Randall was willing to debate whether it was fake or not.

She did admit that she was far from the point of being a professional. While most boys in Iowa started their wrestling careers in second or third grade, this was her first year in the sport. She was the last wrestler in her weight class on the team with her only victory coming from a teammate who had gotten sick. In her 1-12 record, her losses came from nine pins and three by points, 11-8, 9-1, and a 16-0 tech fall.

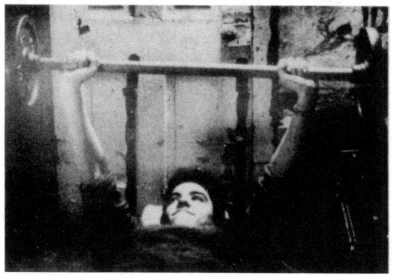

(Randall) Lifting weights at home to build her strength. Photos by John Gaines of the Fairfield Ledger.

She told Johnson, "I have to get faster and stronger. I lift weights and run and I'm trying to do that."

Loerzel also added, "Lisa's biggest problem is that she has to think through all the moves that most good wrestlers naturally do because they've been drilled for so long. She's still thinking everything through, and in wrestling, if you have to think it through, it's already too late."

There were a few hurdles in front of Randall before she could be part of the team. The administration and her parents were supportive of her decision to try. Loerzel said, "She came to me in September and she was pretty serious about it. I told her she'd have to go before the athletic director, the principal and the school board. I sat down with her parents and explained the potential for injuries.

"But I'm here to coach wrestling, not to coach boys or girls. If she'd just been in it for publicity, she'd have been gone in three days, because we work too hard in practice. And she's definitely got the support at home. She's gotten a bloody nose, and she's gotten cracked on pretty good a few times in practice, but nothing serious."

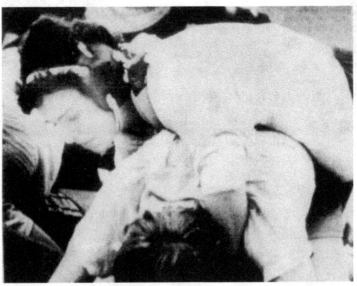

(Randall) Working hard against teammates in practice. Photos by John Gaines of the Fairfield Ledger.

(Randall) Taking a breather at the end of a strenuous workout. Photos by John Gaines of the Fairfield Ledger.

Roberta, Randall's mother, was a little reluctant. She was proud of Randall, but afraid that she might get hurt.

"If that's what she wants," she said, "she should go for it. I try not to discourage my kids — if they want to do something within reason, then I let them try it. My husband Jim is really proud of her, too. He's the athlete in the family, not me. He used to wrestle in high school and he lifts weights with Lisa now. Actually, I was surprised that the school district even let her go out. And I've been surprised at how the boys have treated her — they've been great. Back in my day and age, she'd have been considered an outcast or a tomboy."

Loerzel said he would stop the other wrestlers on his team, all boys, from making things difficult for Randall.

"I've got good kids in this program and they'll do what I say," he explained. "Actually, some of the other students in my classes made a bigger deal of this than my wrestlers did. Oh, some of the less successful wrestlers maybe have been a little bothered by the press that Lisa's gotten, but the best wrestlers don't care. You get in the wrestling room, and you're not up against a girl or a guy for a spot on the team, you're up against another wrestler. And if you want to win, you beat that person, period."

Johnson reported that, when out of the wrestling room, Randall enjoyed cooking and drawing. However, with wrestling practice, homework, meets, and outside training, she had very little time to do other things. Her goals were to make it to the varsity team and, before she graduated, earn a trip to the state tournament.

Loerzel added his thoughts: "That should be every high school wrestler's goal. She's got a long way to go, but if she stays out, who knows? I'm going to sound like a male chauvinist pig, but if it were my daughter, I'd try to talk her out of it, but then my daughter's going to be bigger and she'd just get killed out there. Lisa's advantage is that she's small and she'll probably stay that way. I can see why Lisa wants to do this, and I admire her for it. I don't think she wants to be one of the guys. I don't think there are any big undertones or implications. I think she just wants to be Lisa doing what Lisa wants to do."

***

Dawn Blue joined the Independence High School team in 1989.

Dawn Blue takes a shot on a teammate.
Photo provided by Matthew Shannon.

Girl versus Girl

The first girl on a varsity boys' team came in 1992. However, there wasn't just one earning her spot, there were two and they were both in Eastern Iowa. Stacy Light of Lisbon High School joined the wrestling team alongside her cousin, Ike, who at the time was working toward being Iowa's ninth four-time state champion on a team hunting for their fifteenth state title since becoming a 1A school in 1973.

According to Jeff Johnson of the Cedar Rapids Gazette, the entire school was excited about it. Schoolmates would ask her, "Have you gotten down to your weight yet?" or "Are you ready for Saturday?"

About her first varsity meet, the Keith Young Invitational in Cedar Falls, she said, "I'm kind of nervous about it. I think if I stay in it, I'll probably be able to compete with everyone, but I don't know how I'll do."

Harty of the Iowa High School Athletic Association commented that Light was "far from being the first", however the majority of females on wrestling teams were on the junior high school level. They also didn't see it through for long. A few had strived for a spot on the varsity team but "we don't get many."

He also noted that, while a few states had welcomed girls to join their high school teams, there were just as many that prohibited girls from being in wrestling and football. He then explained that in the state of Iowa the decision fell to the athlete and her family.

Harty said, "If the girl, after being made fully aware of the circumstances, wants to wrestle and her parents allow it, then we are not averse to it."

Light rubs her neck Saturday after she was pinned by Mike Jochmann of Bettendorf in a consolation match at the Keith Young Invitational in Cedar Falls. She was also pinned in the first round. Gazette photos by J. Scott Park

Light's desire to join the team all stemmed from her being questioned in physical education class on joining a winter sport. She decided on wrestling since her brothers and cousins had all been part of the team. Her brother, Vance, was a coach at neighboring Lisbon.

Wrestling was not new to Stacy. She had been part of the sport from first to fifth grade and made it to freestyle nationals in the second grade.

It was that legacy plus the support of her family that confirmed the decision for Light. She told The Gazette, "My parents like it. There's a lot of stuff at home now, since Vance is coaching over at Mount Vernon, about me wrestling against the Mount Vernon guys."

Her brother, Vince, added, ""I don't really have a preference about it. It's her decision. I think she'll win some matches."

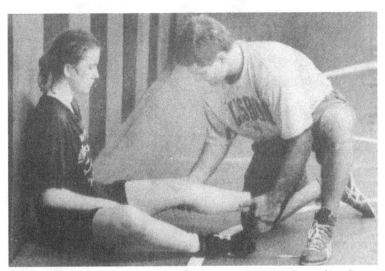

Coach Chris Lembeck checks Light's leg after a hard practice. Gazette photos by J. Scott Park

Light receives congratulations from heavyweight Tony Baltes, middle, and 189-pounder Tait Stamp after a recent workout. Her teammates have welcomed her as a just another member of the team.

Gazette photos by J. Scott Park

What did her friends think? They urged her "Do it, to go for it!"

Coach Chris Lembeck was amenable to Light training with the varsity and brought her in as a part of the team. He was short three weight classes each meet so Light was a welcome addition to the group. Once he consulted with the Iowa High School Athletic Association, he made her the varsity 119-pound starter.

Lembeck told The Gazette, "It's been nothing but a positive experience. All of the wrestlers have been supportive.

Stacy, when she made her decision, made it 100 percent. She hasn't looked back since, and I don't think she will. Obviously, she's a very courageous young lady. She's willing to take a risk and take such a huge challenge. You've got to respect that."

Light, bottom, struggles to fight off the pinning hold applied by Bettendorf's Mike Jochmann in the Keith Young Invitational at Cedar Falls Saturday. She was eventually pinned. Gazette photos by J. Scott Park

The rest of the team was happy to have her in the room as well and treated her like one of them. Light said, "There hasn't been anything negative. They've been real good."

Her teammate, heavyweight Tony Baltes, gave his input about having Light on the team. "I think going in, nobody really knew what to expect. We had never experienced anything like it. At first it was a little different, but now a lot of times you don't even notice there's a girl in the room."

Lembeck added his feelings about Light wrestling for him. "All I expect is for her to wrestle her heart out, each and every match. Just like I expect 100 percent from each one of

28

the guys. If that means losing a match, that's fine and dandy. As long as I know she gave it her all."

With the Light name being predominant in the Lisbon wrestling community, those watching the team also seemed to be on board with a female on the team.

Lembeck said, "It hasn't been as big a deal as I thought it was going to be. For all of the things this program has done and all of the accomplishments that the Light name has underneath its belt, this has barely raised an eyelash or an eyebrow of the people around here."

Lembeck did, however, prepare her for the possibility that her position on the team might not work for everyone. He warned her of guys who would refuse to wrestle her, especially in a dual.

The attention was the last thing Light wanted. Her only desire was to wrestle.

"I don't really look at it as doing it for women," she said. "I look at it as doing it for myself. It's just something I like to do."

Lembeck did have the difficult conversation with Light over any negativity she might encounter. She fully understood what she was facing.

"I think I'm ready for any negative reaction. I think I can handle it pretty well," she said.

Lembeck added, "There very well may be some wrestlers that might not wrestle her. That'll happen. It's not very apt to happen in a tournament, but in a dual-meet situation, I bet we'll come across some people who will choose not to wrestle her. Hey, I'll take the six points. I've been giving enough six-pointers away, I'll be very happy to take one."

At the time the article was published in 1992, no one could predict how Light would do. Her quickness would make up for what knowledge she lacked. However, Lembeck believed she was ready for the competition season and didn't anticipate her getting hurt.

Lisbon wrestler Stacy Light takes down teammate Cameron Schumacher the first day of practice this winter. Light is the first girl to wrestle at Lisbon. Gazette photos by J. Scott Park

"Potentially, I'm going to wait and see. Just as I think she is, and just as I think everybody else is. She's got that natural ability, and that's a huge part of wrestling right there. With hard work, if she works on her strength, she'll be able to win some matches. There's no doubt about that."

Light continued, "Hopefully, I'll end up with a winning record. Getting to the state tournament is something I'd like to do."

Wrestler Stacy Light, center, enjoys her time with four other Lisbon High School sophomores during a night out for pizza in Mount Vernon. At right is Sara Carter. Gazette photos by J. Scott Park

It wasn't long before Light got her first taste of competition. In the same edition of the Gazette were the results of her first competition, the Keith Young Invitational in Cedar Falls December 5th, 1992. She was pinned in less than 25 seconds by Denver's Josh Meier. Her second match against Bettendorf's Mike Jochmann was significantly longer but ended the same way. He ended the match by pin in 3:24.

The Gazette's Johnson reported that both matches left her on the defensive. Although she narrowly avoided the near fall a couple of times before she was pinned in her match against Jochmann, she was behind 10-0 when it ended.

Light understood that it was a difficult competition. She told Johnson, "It's a tough tournament. The second match, I was just trying not to get pinned. I was trying not to get beat as bad as I did before."

Jochmann was impressed by the fight that Light put up against him.

"I think it's just great," he said. "The only objection I have is that if they let girls wrestle, they should let guys play volleyball, too. Other than that, I think it's fantastic. I really didn't think of it much differently. I have a teammate who wrestled a girl back in Bettendorf. I was trying to consider it as just another match. I just went out and did my best to try and beat her."

Both Light and Lembeck were relieved to get the first two matches out of the way and were ready to make improvements to Light's game.

Light concentrates Saturday before her first varsity wrestling match. Light was pinned in the first round of the Keith Young Invitational at Cedar Falls.
Gazette photos by J. Scott Park

Light told the Gazette, "I know not to get down on myself. This was a very tough tournament. This doesn't discourage me."

Lembeck added, "I'm just happy she got her first two matches in. She can only improve from here. Now we can get back in the room and work on some specific things. I'm glad it's over. All of the pressure she had. And the jitters. She wrestled her heart out. I'm proud of her."

At the same time Light was finding her spot on Lisbon's team, Atina Bibbs at Davenport Central was also earning a place on her varsity wrestling team.

All those involved on Central's Blue Devils' team reinforced the love Bibbs had for the sport. She had no intention of bringing a spotlight to the team.

Bibbs told the Quad City Times, "Last year, I began thinking about wrestling while I was playing basketball. I enjoyed basketball, but wrestling has always been a part of me. By the time school rolled around in the fall, I decided I would go out for wrestling. I told my dad about my decision - he never pushed me into going out - and I started lifting to get into shape."

Mel Bibbs knew there would be some controversy with his daughter wrestling for him at Central, especially since she was a recent transfer from Davenport North.

He said, "I told her coming in that I wouldn't treat her any differently than any of our other wrestlers. In fact, she would probably have to put forth a 110 percent effort, if for no other reason she is the coach's kid. She had a two year layoff from the sport, and like anything, it's going to take some time for her to get back into wrestling shape. I think you'll see her make steady progress."

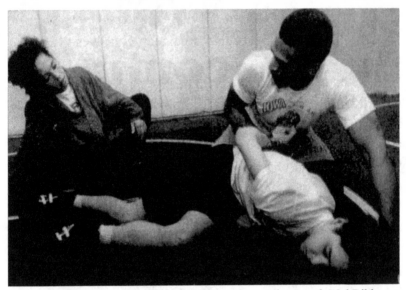

Atina Bibbs looks on as her father, Central wrestling coach Mel Bibbs, shows her proper technique on a Blue Devil teammate. Photo taken by Greg Boll of the Quad City Times.

Other schools in the area showed their support by making arrangements for Bibbs.

Coach Bibbs said, "Last week, when we were at Bettendorf for the double dual, they provided a separate locker room for her so that was no problem. For weigh-ins, we had a school nurse present to do it for Atina. If necessary, wrestlers are allowed to get down to their 'birthday suits' to make weight. We didn't want that to become a problem."

Nerves got to Bibbs before the Bettendorf meet.

She told the Times, "During class last Thursday, my stomach was grumbling all day and it wasn't because I was hungry. It continued while I was warming up. The two teams knew that I was going to be wrestling so it wasn't a surprise to them. Someone from North told me before the match, 'It's good to see you back on the mat again.'"

Bibbs lost both of her 110-pound varsity matches to Bettendorf and Davenport North.

One of her Central teammates, Billy Westmoreland, had faced Bibbs in junior high. "I know she beat me twice in seventh grade by scores of 2-0 and 9-6 before I finally beat her 4-3." He compared her success then to her work in Central's wrestling room.

"Right now, she's not physically strong as you probably need to be, but maybe by mid-season she'll have the necessary strength. Some people from outside ask me about her wrestling on our team. I tell them that she's not out there for the publicity; she's probably had more matches already than most of the guys on our team. I think everybody on our team had accepted her; she's not getting special favors. We all run and

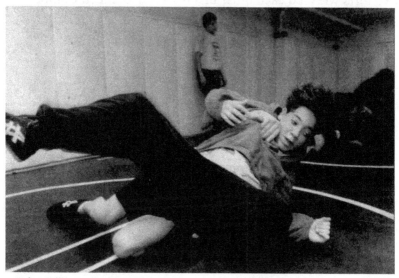

Atina Bibbs, who is wrestling for Central this season, works out during a team practice. The junior has extensive wrestling experience. Photo taken by Greg Boll of the Quad City Times

lift together, and go through the usual wrestling workouts. Hopefully she can help us start winning some more meets."

Support for Bibb's continued through Davenport Central.

"Last week, teachers were asking me if I could eat or if I need to lose weight," Bibbs said. "The teachers, plus other students and friends were wishing me good luck in my matches. Last summer during softball (where she caught and played shortstop with North before transferring to Central), I weighed about 125. When I started serious training, I was at about 120 so those last six or eight pounds was tough coming off."

Light and Bibbs faced off in a dual that season at George Marshall gym. It was the first time in Iowa history that two girls wrestled each other in a high school meet. Competing at 112 pounds, Bibbs won the match 14-5.

Dualing Teams

A year later in 1993, four girls found a spot on Cedar Rapids Kennedy's wrestling team. According to The Gazette's Jeff Johnson, freshman Katie Sampica, sophomore Danielle Ruhberg, junior Kiya Arnold-Arons and senior Becky Carver joined Rick Blackwell's junior varsity. They were one of the only squads to have multiple females as team members.

Blackwell had the first clue that a girl might join them when Arnold-Arons confessed that she was interested in wrestling. She wanted to stay fit by practicing. Sampica and Ruhberg followed in their brothers' footsteps, who also wrestled at Kennedy.

Blackwell was excited to have them in the room. "They're wonderful. The great thing about it is that they lost 11 or 12 matches in a JV tournament in Belle Plaine last weekend, but every one of them came to practice Monday morning. They wanted to learn more, and that's all you can ask as a coach."

Sampica had the only win in Belle Plaine.

Blackwell said, "The good thing is that they are not trying to prove anything. They just wanted to try wrestling to see if they liked it. It's been a great experience for everybody."

The four female Kennedy grapplers had the approval and support of all those in the wrestling room. There was only one male teammate who was reluctant to compete against a girl.

Blackwell told the Gazette, "They want to learn. They hate to lose, but they understand that physically and skill-wise they are behind the guys simply because they haven't wrestled before."

The girls inspired Blackwell to hope that his own 5th grade daughter would join the Cougar team in the future. He felt that more girls would join his squad in the next few years. "I really hope they stick with it."

***

Saber Wrestling Statistics

Name: Megan Peavey
Grade: 9
Other Activities: FFA, FCA, Volleyball, Softball, Band, Chorus, Speech, Student Council, Class President.
Favorite Food: Everything
Favorite Book: True Confessions of Charlotte Doyle

What I remembered most about the 1994-95 Wrestling Season: The first day of practice and the Billy Baroo.

Wrestling Specialty: Headgear fashion and dresses for weigh-ins.

1994-95 Statistics

Categories	Varsity For/Against	JV For/Against	Freshman for/Against
Takedowns	0-1	0-2	
Reversals	0-0	0-0	
Escapes	1-0	1-0	
Total nearfall	0-0	0-1	
Penalties	0-0	0-0	
Total points	1	1	
Pins	0	0	
Technical falls	0	0	

Varsity Record: 0-4
JV Record: 0-2
Freshman Record:
Conference Record: 0-4
Career Record: 0-4   Letter Points: 0

Comments: This was definitely a new experience for everyone involved. As far as I was concerned, it ended up being a very positive one as well. Although we never did get those wins out of the 103 lb. spot, the ability for us to adjust to this situation was one of those experiences which I feel taught everyone a lot about ourselves, and showed me we've got a great group of kids here at Central. After her initial Indoctrination, Mean (or was it Jessica?) became another member of the team. Mean didn't score many points, but the hard fought escapes are something which will be remembered for a long time, along with her guts of getting off of her back. Mean was a member of the 3.0 Club...thanks for the effort.

The stat sheet listing Megan Peavey as "Mean" Peavey.
Photo provided by Kurt Kreiter

38

According to Kurt Kreiter, athletic director at Central Dewitt High School, another girl made her way onto the varsity team a couple years later. Megan Peavey was the first girl to wrestle for Central Dewitt and earned the nickname "Mean" by a typo in her stats. During her freshman year, she earned a point for an escape. Kreiter, who was the wrestling coach at the time, said, "I wanted to coach a girl before I retire, and now I can say that I have."

Megan Peavey wrestles for Central Dewitt. Photo by Brett McKamey

***

While girls in Iowa were finding their way onto the mat, girls were fighting to get their opportunity elsewhere in the United States. In 1996, that the high school officials organization in Texas disbanded after being served a lawsuit for discrimination when officials refused to officiate a boy versus girl match.

John Rizzuti, president of the Texas Wrestling Officials Association, said, "They can't make us do this. Hell will freeze over before I officiate girls being brutalized by boys."

Two Texas female wrestlers joined with the American Civil Liberties Union to leverage the suit against the officials association. The disbandment was the counter move to stall the lawsuit.

However, the mothers of wrestlers Rai Barnett and Karen Herring responded with a suit of their own, citing discrimination against their daughters. In their claim, they included both the officials association and the Texas Interscholastic Wrestling Association as the wrongdoers. This was done because there was proof that the officials association was still intact.

The discrimination lawsuit demanded that the wrestlers and their families receive $10,000. It also required that the Wrestling Association and the officials association be forced to allow girls to wrestle. At this time, there were twenty girl wrestlers in Texas.

* * *

In 2001, the first girls dual meet in Iowa history happened in Gilbert, Iowa between Gilbert High School and Spencer High School. According to The Predicament, the teams were formed by school clubs. Gilbert's team was coached by Scott Auderer and Spencer's by Dave Storm. They practiced two mornings and two evenings during the week for two months before they faced each other on February 4, 2001. Spencer won 43-19. There were eleven varsity matches followed by twenty-five exhibition match-ups.

Although the girls were not on the boys team recognized by the IHSAA, they belonged to school clubs to compete against the other team. They hoped to have a rematch a few weeks later in Spencer.

Dave Storm, the Spencer girls dual coach, told the authors of this book how his team came to be. "I took my daughter to a USGWA tournament over in Gilbert when she was in fourth grade. She wasn't eligible to wrestle so I got

Spencer High School's girls dual team. Photo provided by Dave Storm.

some information. We went the next year to the Gilbert tournament, and she was in fifth grade. I watched some of the high school girls that were wrestling. And Gilbert had a team at that time.

"After the tournament was over, they had an announcement that all coaches got together and they said, 'Hey, why don't we start having a bunch of us coaches start getting more girls out like Gilbert has and we can start having duals around the state' I thought the rest of the coaches were going to do that, so I did it and got a bunch of girls out."

Then he and Auderer scheduled the dual meet in February 2001.

"We had the dual meet in Gilbert," Storm said, "and The Predicament was there and Les Anderson from Iowa State (coach) was there and it was a lot of fun. And, you know, I told my girls right before the meet in the locker room after we warmed up. I said, 'You know what? You girls are going to make history in Iowa." I said, 'You are going to be the very first girls to ever dual another town in Iowa.' "

Storm explained what he did to put his Spencer team together. "I went out to the USGWA national tournament with my daughter... I took my video camera out there and I just videotaped - videotape, videotape, videotape - all these different girls, high school girls, middle school, collegiate girls wrestling. Then the next year, when I went to get my team together, I just put up a bunch of posters around the school for girls interested in going out for all girls wrestling, not wrestling boys. We're not going to wrestle - I just kept stressing - not wrestling boys and kind of learning a little bit of self-defense along with it.

"I told my wife, 'If I have 10 girls show up at the meeting, you know, I'll be surprised.' I ended up having probably well over 30, close to 40, girls that showed up to the meeting."

Once he had potential wrestlers interested in joining, he reached out to their families to get support as well.

"I ... had them bring in their parents and talk to them about how physical wrestling was and doing moves and stuff like that. I got parent backing behind me. It worked out well. I ended up having, I think it was, 26 girls on my first high school wrestling team."

What was his takeaway about that historical meet?

Spencer used this graphic to recruit girls for their girls dual team.
Photo provided by Dave Storm

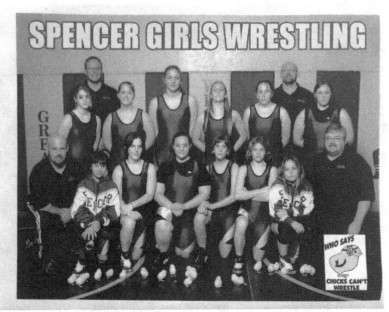

Spencer's official team photo taken by... Photo provided by Dave Storm

Storm said, "It was just fun because it was us against Gilbert. It was a team competition. What was fun about it was ... I had girls that were athletes, girls that were not athletes, girls that this was the first athletic thing that they ever did. From all mixes and they all came together as a team. And man, we were cheering and screaming and hollering and having a great time. I think there was actually a news channel there and interviewed a couple of the girls too."

***

Early in 2004, Iowa had its first high school girl wrestler get a win at a district meet heading to the state championship. Cindy Johnson, a freshman at West Burlington High School, one of the few girls in the state to participate in wrestling that year, was a member of the varsity. Others were Karla Wood and Jordan Brenchley of Mount Pleasant.

Matt Levins of the Hawk Eye reported that Johnson was very talented at the sport, touting a winning 12-8 record as she prepared for the SEI Superconference Tournament at WACO High School in Wayland, Ia. Five of those wins came via pin.

Johnson told Levins, "Things are going really well so far. My coaches keep my confidence up and they push me to the limit. They treat me just like anybody else in the practice room. They don't cut me any slack.

"My first year of varsity has been hard. It's taking an extra step from junior high. Now you're wrestling men, not little boys."

Her coach, Mike Sayre, commented, "Cindy is a good technician. She does real well for a freshman. She works just as hard as the boys do. She's doing extremely well for being a young wrestler and being a girl."

Like many female wrestlers in Iowa, the sport ran in her blood. Her older sister, Cathy, was the first girl to wrestle for the team. John Johnson, her father, helped bring the wrestling program into existence. Her brothers, Christopher and Chad, were both on the team when they were in high school, with Chris taking third twice at the state meet.

Johnson told Levins, "When I was in first grade, my brothers both wrestled in the Burlington Kids Club. When I was in second grade, I told my dad I wanted to wrestle. Coach Sayre and Coach (Jim) Drain were my main coaches. They know my entire family.

"My sister Cathy wrestled her junior and senior years. It was just like an older image of me. I always watched her on the mat and thought, 'That's going to be me some day.' It takes a lot of courage. I'm really proud of her. Being a girl, you take a lot of stuff from the guys, whether they mean it or not."

Watching her family compete gave her a jump start in wrestling. Before she hit middle school, she had already taken first at state and nationals and was runner-up in the world championships. This performance was seen in her only home double dual for West Burlington that year when she boosted the team to a 6-0 start in each bout with wins over both other schools.

"Some of them think, 'Oh, she's a girl. She won't be much of a match.'," Johnson said. "After they wrestle me, they know I am someone who knows what they are doing. They think, 'This girl has some talent. I shouldn't cut her any slack. She knows how to wrestle.' "

About the double dual, she said, "That was big. A lot of my friends were there and it was Parents Night. The coaches really wanted to dominate them. It started off at 103 and we wanted to get out to a lead. It was very contagious. When your teammates see you win, they want to keep it going. You have confidence and they have confidence.

"When I beat a boy, I feel like I've done good. But I don't want them to quit. I've had that happen. 'Oh no, a girl beat me.' When I beat somebody, I feel really good about myself."

She earned the respect of both her coaches and teammates after that meet. Sayre told the Hawkeye, "She really took it to the Davis County kid (Colton Taylor). She took it to the Van Buren boy (Dexter Dick), too. She wrestled extremely well and with a lot of intensity. She got third place in the Van Buren tournament and that really helped her a lot confidence-wise.

"It's a lot of fun to have her in the practice room. The boys really respect her. We push her just as hard as we push the boys. We pound on her just as hard as we do with the other kids. After a while, she is just part of the team, just another wrestler on the team."

Watching her brother, Christopher, compete in Des Moines at the state meet gave Johnson the aspiration to do the same thing. Ashley Pender of Colfax-Mingo was the first to qualify for the district meet.

If she did make it to Des Moines, Bud Lego, the IHSAA information specialist, informed the Hawk Eye, "As far as dressing and weighing in, she will use the room where the cheerleaders dress. Allocations would be made for her, suitable for her and respectful of her."

Rick Willow, IHSAA assistant executive director, added, "We'd welcome her. We'd make her feel welcome and make whatever provisions are necessary to accommodate her."

Johnson was quoted as saying about the state tournament, "Maybe some year I can do it. Then the boys would give me a lot more respect."

Johnson was already taking different measures from what the guys did. The Hawk Eye explained that she wore a hair net and sports bra during each match and had to be accompanied by a female associate from the home facility when she weighed in. She was also assigned a separate place to change before competing.

When she was off the mat, she was like others girls. She enjoyed attending school, went shopping, and spent time with friends and family. She also played softball, ran on the track team, and rode horses.

In February 2004, Johnson became the first girl in Class 1A or 2A to win a match at an Iowa high school district championship, pinning her opponent in her second round bout.

Making It To the State Meet

Chandra Peterson started with the Lake Mills High School team also in 2004 and completed all four years with them with a record of 54-53. Her opponents didn't take well to losing to her.

In a later interview she said, "As far as my teammates, some were really great and supportive of me and some not so much. I actually had one of the wrestlers who used to really lay it on thick when we were in high school apologize to me a few years ago.

"He apologized that he wasn't more inclusive and didn't always treat me the best. I thought that was really nice. Frankly, the teasing and being left out of things wasn't what bothered me the most. What bothered me was how dismissive the guys were of my accomplishments in the girls world.

"For example, my junior year I took 5th at Fargo freestyle nationals and became an All-American – the guys were really dismissive of what was a huge accomplishment. Coach Burns actually put my picture in the school trophy case, which was so cool, and a lot of my teammates made it really clear to me they didn't think he should have put it there because I was just wrestling other girls, which they saw as lesser than the boys competitions."

She participated in sectionals with the varsity but couldn't quite move on to divisionals.

When speaking to Peterson, she explained why she decided to wrestle. "It's actually a funny story. I was really little, so I don't know exactly what it was that made me WANT to wrestle. My brother is two years younger than me. He wrestled when he was in kindergarten and he started again his first grade year, and after a few tournaments, he decided he was going to 'retire.'

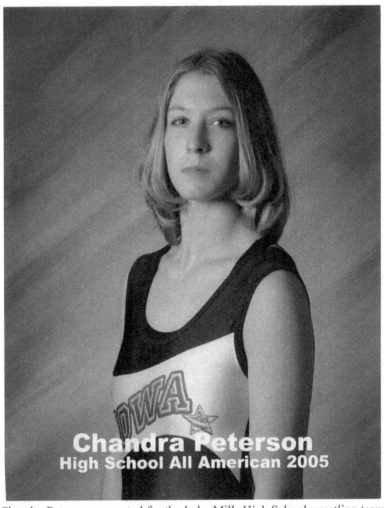

Chandra Peterson competed for the Lake Mills High School wrestling team beginning in 2004. Photo provided by Bill Byrnes.

"I had really wanted to join and had been begging my parents to let me try it, but I was in dance at the time and they kept telling me no. After my brother decided to 'retire,' my parents decided that they would let me wrestle, in an attempt to keep him involved in the sport. I was in third grade at the time and I fell in love with the sport. By the time sixth grade rolled around, my mom made me decide between dance and wrestling and it wasn't a contest. I wanted to keep wrestling because I loved it so much."

She related her experiences during her high school wrestling career. "I LOVE Coach Burns, but I don't know that he was thrilled about the idea of me joining the team when I first started. In the end, I know he nominated me for awards, stuck up for me at tournaments and supported me when I was struggling my senior year with weight management. I'd like to think I proved his assumptions wrong, but I don't know what those were and I've never actually asked him. Everyone always had an opinion about how far I would make it. I started wrestling in third grade and when I was starting I heard a lot of 'Oh that's great that you are doing it now, but you will never make it in middle school because the boys will be stronger and tougher.'

"In middle school, I dominated – had one of the best records on the team, if not the best honestly. All through middle school I got the same thing though – 'That's great but you will never make it in high school.' And then I wrestled varsity all four years.

"I loved our dual meets at home. We would turn the lights off in the gym except one giant spotlight on the mat. We would all run out to some theme song every time – one year we ran out to AC/DC "Back in Black." My parents never missed a meet or tournament – they were ALWAYS there. I have lots of memories from practices. Coach always told us that the shape we were in for wrestling would be the best shape we would ever be in our lives. I think he was right.

I have memories of conditioning that I will probably never forget. I cut weight pretty hard as well so I have a lot of memories of being thirsty.

"I oddly also remember less about my matches than I do some of the weird accommodations schools would set up for me. Lots of times I would just be put in the cheerleading room (with no ability to shower b/c they were never in a locker room). Sometimes, they would have a teacher's room open for me to put my stuff in and change. One time I had what was essentially a closet to change and keep my bag. If I wanted to shower before we left, I would have to beg a teammate to clear out their locker room and stand guard while I showered so no one would come in. They always had to find a woman to weigh me in."

Peterson was a four-year letter winner for Lake Mills. Outside of the high school wrestling room, she was an All-American in 2006, The Mat 2006 All American Girls Wrestling Team Honorable Mention, a USGWA National Champion in 2003, five-time USGWA Iowa state champion; and the Iowa Wrestling Federation women's athlete of the year as a sophomore. She now coaches wrestling herself in California.

In that same year, women's freestyle wrestling made its debut in the Summer Olympics. Sara McMann brought home the silver medal in the 55-63kg division and Patricia Miranda won bronze in the 48kg division. The team was coached by Terry Steiner.

* * *

In 2011, Cassy Herkelman of Cedar Falls High School, went to the state tournament and was the first female wrestler to be victorious in a match. According to ESPN.com, this happened when her opponent, Joel Northrup of Linn-Mar High School, forfeited instead of facing her. The decision, which Northrup based on religious beliefs and the theory that it wasn't right to face off against a girl, caught the nation's attention. Northrup was a contender for the 112-pound championship.

Herkelman was quoted by ESPN.com as saying "He had the right to make his own choice, and he made his choice. It's not like he did what he didn't want to do."

Her father, Bill Herkelman, added, "That's their belief, and I praise them for sticking to it. This is the biggest stage in wrestling in the state, I would say, and they stuck to their beliefs when it probably tested it the most. It was probably a tough pill for him to swallow."

Cassy had a different idea about the situation.

"It would be a 'lot more fun and exciting' if girls could wrestle other girls in Iowa instead of having to face boys," she told ESPN.

Her teammate, David Langley, who had experience wrestling girls, said, "With all the pressure she had on her, I thought she did pretty good. She handled it pretty well and didn't let it get to her head or anything."

Herkelman lost her next two matches, ending her season that year at 21-15.

The other girl at the meet in 2011, Megan Black of Ottumwa High School, lost both her matches on the first day of the tournament. Herkelman and Black share the honor as the first two girls to make it to the Iowa state wrestling meet.

The next year, in 2012, Megan Black took her spot in wrestling history as being the first girl to win a medal at the Iowa State High School Wrestling tournament.

During her junior year, Black changed schools to Eddyville-Blakesburg to get a more specialized education towards her career of choice. "I knew in my future I wanted to be in agriculture. I loved it at Ottumwa. They have great kids there and I enjoyed wrestling there, but they didn't have any agriculture classes there. Eddyville-Blakesburg has an amazing agriculture program, one of the best in the state. I want to come back and take over the family farm someday. So I transferred to Eddyville-Blakesburg to study agriculture."

This, of course, meant that she now wrestled for Eddyville-Blakesburg. After another successful season, she found herself back in Des Moines to wrestle for a state medal.

This was the point where she won her first match, making her the first girl to win a match at the state meet in which she actually wrestled. It was also the year that she claimed her eighth place medal. She told the Predicament, "It was always my personal goal to place at state and be up on the stand. It felt great seeing all the hard work I had put in had paid off. At that moment I felt like any other wrestler who gets on the podium. You feel good about what you have done."

Black explained how she and her family were treated by fans who felt she didn't belong on the mat with the boys. Negative words were said. Things were thrown at them as they passed, not just at state but everywhere.

"One time at the state tournament some guy came up to my Mom and said, 'You ought to make her go to church and read the Bible.' They don't even know that I am a Christian. I give all the glory to God. He is the One who makes all this possible. Those kind of comments used to hurt me, but I realize that they don't even know who I really am. I don't think I am any different from any other wrestler, but some fans do look at me differently. It takes those negative people to make me stronger. At the end of the day, it doesn't really matter what they say. I've had a lot of people stand by me and help me through all this. They are the ones who know that I'm not in this sport to wrestle boys. I'm doing this because I love wrestling and because I want to be the best that I can be."

Yahoo Sports reported that after the move to Eddyville-Blakesburg, she returned to Des Moines and won the first competitive match wrestled by a female in history when she beat Jacob Schmidt of Don Bosco, 10-0. She lost her next bout, then was victorious in the third.

Unfortunately a separated collarbone in the third match stopped her year, giving her eighth place, a spot on the podium and a state medal, "something I've been waiting for a long time," she said.

Black explained the injury as, "I just kind of rolled over it and I felt a couple of pops. There's always next year."

Her father, Matt Black, added, "It's not a novelty act anymore. You remember all the people who told her to quit - former coaches who told her, 'Just quit. You'll never get any better.' But she got better."

However, the road to the podium wasn't smooth for Black.

She related her journey to the online wrestling publication, The Predicament, on December 30, 2013.

"When I first started wrestling in third grade, I never thought of myself as any different from anyone else. No one told me I couldn't do what my teammates were doing. No one treated me any different than anyone else. I never thought of myself as a female wrestler. I always just thought of myself as a wrestler. That's all I ever wanted to be. I think that's what made me who I am today. Everybody treated me the same as anyone else."

As she grew older and wrestled more, matches became more and more difficult, especially when she hit high school in Ottumwa.

"I never really thought of myself being a girl," Black said. "I was definitely nervous being on the varsity. I was wrestling some good kids now, so I was more nervous."

That anxiety was magnified when she and Herkelman made it to the state meet in her sophomore year. She told the Predicament, "It was quite an eye-opening experience for me, There were a lot of reporters, a lot of people. I tried to put all that out of my mind and just focus on wrestling, but it was hard. My parents and my coaches kept me focused on wrestling and the things I could control."

About Herkelman's controversial win and the resulting national attention, Black said, "I didn't realize until after the meet that everyone was focused on her and not me. It kind of hurt in a way.

"But in a way it was good for me. I didn't have the spotlight as much as Cassy did."

She also said about the state meet, "The people at Wells Fargo did a great job. They helped keep people away from me. (They) gave me a special place where I could go to be alone and just get away from everybody and everything going on and just try to stay focused on wrestling."

She had trouble staying healthy and staying in a weight class her senior year. She did not make it to the individual state meet but did get two wins by pins at the State Dual Meet. Her final loss of her high school career was to Hunter Washburn of Alburnett, who beat her with a pin.

"It was sad after my last match,' she said. "It was hard to watch the next few days. My next goal is to become an Olympic champion. I want to do the best I can for my country. I want to thank everyone who made me the person I am today. I want to thank my parents, my brother (Tucker) and sister (Maddie), my coaches and teammates and especially God. It's been a great ride. Hopefully there is much more to come."

***

In 2014, Dike-New Hartford's Anna Poyner was a senior letter winner. She was also voted captain by her team.

Anne Poyner poses with the State Dual trophy.
Photo provided by Tony Norton.

Three years later in 2017, Iowa saw their first bracket made up entirely of girls at in the 113-lb. weight class at the Centerville Big Red JV tournament at the Lakeville Gymnasium.

Morgan Lawson, a wrestler for Ottumwa High School, told the Ottumwa Courier, "We're all going to be wrestling at 113. I've been kind of run down because I've been cutting weight, but I feel like I'll be at a more comfortable weight and, once I get some food in my body, I'm going to wrestle really well."

Her coach, Jeremy Frueh, said, "I know Morgan's excited for the opportunity and we're excited for her."

This event spurred talk of a girls Iowa State Wrestling Tournament in the near future, with a meeting between Jean Berger of the Iowa Girls High School Athletic Union and Alan Bese of the Iowa High School Athletic Association happening later that winter.

When asked about the possibility of an all-girls tournament, Lawson said, "When I first saw that, I thought it would be amazing. It would be great for girls to be able to go and compete against each other for a state title. I'd be really excited to be one of those girls that could get to compete in that. We could all grapple together and show everyone that wrestling isn't just a sport for guys."

Frueh added, "I think it will probably take some time to put together, but for someone like Morgan that would be a tremendous opportunity. She's improved a lot over the last two years no matter who she's had to face. I think we're trending towards the state having something like a female state wrestling tournament. There's enough people involved in it. It'll be interesting to see what they do.

Ottumwa's Morgan Lawson Is one of approximately 80 female competitors that are participating on high school wrestling teams around the state of Iowa. The increase in female participation has opened the possibility of an Iowa Girls State Wrestling Tournament sometime in the future.
Photo by Scott Jackson of the Ottumwa Courier.

"I would assume the girls would have to continue working out with the guys. I don't quite think there's enough female participation yet for a school to have its own female wrestling team. I think it would be fun. There's certainly an interest among the female student athletes to come out for the sport. I think, if a state tournament was made available, that would only continue to the increase in those numbers."

He continued his thoughts on the benefit of the meet. "I think there are some parents out there that shy away from letting their kids compete if it's females competing with males in the sport right now. If there was a state tournament made

59

available, I think you'd see an incredible increase in female participation."

At that point, there were 80-100 girls wrestling throughout the state of Iowa.

The Ogden Meet

It was a frigid morning in January when the next vital step in high school girls wrestling in the state of Iowa happened just shy of a year later in Ogden, Iowa.

A month earlier, a notice appeared on social media about a girls only division being held at the Ogden High School JV Tournament on January 6th, 2018.

An invitation went out to all the high schools in the state, asking for their girls to attend. It was echoed on social media in groups administered by Jason Loyd of Iowa AAU Wrestling and Charlotte Bailey of Iowa USA Wrestling.

The message was specific: If the girls wanted to wrestle other girls in high school, they needed to be at this event.

Teams streamed into the Ogden gym early that morning with fans and wrestlers filling the stands. The floor was filled with boys warming up for the day. One girl wrestler could be observed getting ready among them. Two mats were set up in the main gymnasium and one nearly took up the capacity of the cafeteria.

It wasn't long before the gymnasium filled with wrestlers, parents, cheerleaders, and coaches.

The JV boy wrestlers were called to weigh in first, then the girls. The group of female wrestlers found their way to the doorway leading outside, eyeing the ten-foot sidewalk that separated the main school building and the pole building that housed the wrestling room. It took little while for them to summon the courage to sprint the short distance in the frigid cold. This was the first opportunity for the eleven girls to get to know each other as they discussed if there was another route to take. Finally, there were a couple shrieks and a few giggles as they hurried together from one building to the other. Their coaches and a few parents chuckled as they followed. The girls were pleasantly surprised to find the wrestling building where the weigh-ins were held was pleasantly warm.

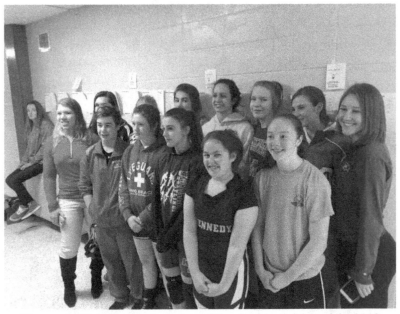

Photos are taken between matches of the all-girls division of the 2018 Ogden meet. Photo taken by Tricia Andersen.

Out of the 91 high school female wrestlers in the state of Iow, eleven girls weighed in for the meet. They included Shae Muecke of Kingsley-Pierson High School, Keagan King and Hannah Payne of South Central-Calhoun, Maddy Buffman and Olivia Diggins of Logan Magnolia, Kim Hendrian of Roland-Story, Llia Hostetter of Colfax Mingo, Chloe Krebsbach and Kate Mostek of Osage, Camrae Schakel of Nevada, and Ali Andersen of Cedar Rapids Kennedy. While almost all of the participants were only an hour or so away,

Andersen was the only girl from the east section of the state to compete.

Krebsbach and Muecke competed in the 113 weight class with Krebsbach taking first after winning two matches. Payne won three matches against Andersen in the 120 bracket, taking first. The 128 weight bracket had five wrestlers in it, King, Diggins, Mostek, Hendrian, and Hostetter. After four rounds, Hendrian finished first, Diggins second, King third, Hostetter fourth, and Mostek fifth. The final bracket of 138 held Buffman and Schakel. Buffman took first in two rounds.

After the first two rounds, activity was stopped to recognize the eleven girls on the mat. Applause resounded from the crowd in response. Television cameras and reporters lined the mats to get the female wrestlers in action. A group picture of the eleven was taken outside in the hall after their first match.

Jesse Sundell, the wrestling coach at Ogden High School, was interviewed by the Des Moines Register. The article appeared three days later on Jan. 9.

"The idea started with our former coach, Brian Reimers. He has been trying to help push to get girls wrestling more involved in the state tournament," Sundell said. "He had mentioned about trying to host our own all-girls tournament. He put me in touch with (Iowa/USA Wrestling Women's Director) Charlotte Bailey. From there I organized and set it up with the help of Charlotte."

He added, "I felt the tournament went well and the wrestlers were very happy and proud of the day. We seemed to get very good reception and recognition from it. Everyone that was there was very happy to see us put the event on in hopes for more success in the future."

Lewis Curtis, Director of Officials for the Iowa High School Athletic Association was quoted by IA Wrestle concerning the Ogden girls only division, "We are excited that Ogden High School has created a separate division for girls in their upcoming tournament. It will be interesting to see the numbers of girls that participate from our member schools, and the reaction we get from the tournament directors. We are very interested in finding ways to increase participation in the sport of wrestling, for boys as well as girls."

Matt Watters of IA Wrestle added, "It is hard to believe how much growth we are seeing in women's wrestling nationwide. I think the importance of this tournament is that it shows other schools in Iowa that we don't have to wait for a governing body to sanction girls wrestling. This shows that going forward, any school may include a girl's division as part of their tournament and give the girls the opportunity to compete against other girls. I would love to eventually see a girls division as part of the state wrestling championships."

Troy Greder, the girls coach at South-Central Calhoun, cornered King and Payne. He had also made arrangements with Kingsley-Pierson and Muecke's parents to coach her also. He also took a moment to talk to Andersen as well about a match.

He saw the importance of that meet in Ogden. "Impact, I think it finally was that glimpse of light for the girls who had been wrestling boys their entire career. I think it showed them that what they had been doing was worth it and that a giant step towards getting sanctioned wrestling in Iowa has been accomplished.

"The growth of girls wrestling is really outstanding," he continued, "The first year I coached Keagan, we had 66 girls in the State Wrestling which was important because it broke the

50 girl mark. We are up to 500 plus now. Really, without being sanctioned we have what almost every sanctioned state has - girl divisions at tournaments, a state Tournament, and we are starting to see Duals. We are just scratching the surface and still have coaches and schools dragging their feet. I don't think we need to rush things and get unneeded road blocks. If we continue to see the growth there won't be a choice, Iowa will have to sanction. The girls Union was started because many believed basketball was too physical for girls to play competitively. I hope they remember their roots and help these girls out."

Ali Andersen and Hannah Payne face off during their match.
Photo taken by Tricia Andersen.

As far as the attention that the girls' division garnered, he said, "I was pleasantly surprised by the coverage, but it should have been covered. It was historic."

His final thoughts on the day were, "I don't know what my fondest memory was, but I saw girls gain a lot of confidence. I saw smiles, win or lose. I saw friendships started. It was a very important day. One I will always remember."

Shae Muecke shared her favorite moment of the historical day. "My favorite memory of the day was just being able to wrestle another girl! Also it was the first time Keagan and I got to compete at a competition together which made it extra special."

Keagan King also shared her favorite memory. "So my favorite part of the day were all the girls there. I have never seen that many girls at a guys tournament in my life. It was so cool to see all of them come together and grow such an amazing sport we call wrestling."

Having the attention of the news media as well as the crowd in the gym was unnerving.

"I tried not to let the cameras get to me," King said, "but I think at the end of the day they did. Just knowing that people are going to be seeing this in a couple days is kind of nerve-racking but I made sure it didn't affect my matches to come. The atmosphere was definitely a positive and exciting one. If you look back at the pictures you see a lot of people in the stands watching the girls wrestle and just in awe that something like that is happening."

Andersen said that she was taken aback to look up and find a camera in her face while she was grappling with Payne.

Muecke also commented on the energy of the day. "At first I was super nervous for the whole thing but after I soaked it in and realized how special this tournament was. It made me even more excited to compete! The atmosphere was crazy awesome."

Andersen grabs a drink of water after a match in the all-girls division at Ogden. Photo taken by Tricia Andersen.

King, Andersen and Muecke saw the long term importance of the Ogden meet that they were a part of.

Muecke said, "I think that meet helped a lot of people realize that girls really do belong on the mat. After that tournament, so many opportunities continued to happen and more girls divisions kept popping up. I think it helped a lot of girls realize that they could be on the mat too.

"That meet was the start," King added. "Without that meet I feel like we wouldn't have the numbers we do two years later. It definitely helped grow women's wrestling and get everyone's attention that GIRLS WRESTLE TOO."

Bonds have formed between the eleven participants of that girls-only division in Ogden.

"Almost all the girls there that day were new people to me but two years later I keep up to date with almost all of them. They are now part of my wrestling family and I will always have that special connection with all of them. They are my sisters (blood or not) and I love them and wish them all good luck for years to come," King said in 2020.

Muecke, interviewed about Ogden, said, "Before that meet, I had only ever practiced with Keagan. I didn't wrestle any of the other girls there before that day. The bonds I made that day were unreal. One of the girls, Chloe, who I actually wrestled that day *(in Ogden),* is my teammate/sister now. Keagan and I now wrestle in college together too and have never been closer. Of course my bond with Ali (Andersen) is crazy close. She's like a little sister to me. I think knowing that we helped pave a way for a lot of girls in years to come is something special that all of us will always hold close to us."

***

The following Saturday on January 13, 2018, Independence High School held the second all-girls division in Iowa high school history. This time, eight girls faced each other. Three – Hendrian, Eliman and Andersen – had been at Ogden the week before. The others were Hannah Michael of Union High School, Tateum Park of Davenport North, Chloe Krebsbach, Hannah Cree of Roland-Story, and Alisha Smith of Pleasant Valley.

Wrestlers pose for a photo at the all-girls division at Independence in 2018.
Photo taken by Tricia Andersen.

Michael, Park, and Krebsbach wrestled in the first bracket with Park taking first, Krebsbach second, and Michael third. In the second bracket there were matches between Hendrian, Eliman, and Andersen with Hendrian placing first, Eliman second, and Andersen third. The last bracket was Cree versus Smith with Smith winning both matches and Cree taking second.

***

Felicity Taylor of South Winneshiek was the first female wrestler in Iowa to win over a hundred matches. This happened during her senior season in 2018. However, wrestling wasn't her first choice as a freshman when she started during the 2014-2015 season.

When she was asked what brought her to the wrestling room, Taylor said, "I had wanted to be on the wrestling cheerleading team. But unfortunately, I didn't make the team, which was really surprising to me at first because I had done gymnastics since I was four years old. I could tumble and I was a small … I was weighing 100 pounds around that time so I just thought I would be a good flyer. I just kind of expected to be on the team. So when I wasn't, I was heartbroken. And I honestly was confused."

Taylor had particular reasons why she wanted to be busy during the winter. She had run cross country and track and wanted to continue to be active. After trying basketball and basketball cheerleading, but didn't like either one.

It was then that she thought about wrestling because her brothers had wrestled and she was familiar with it while growing up.

"My younger brother, I was his practice dummy. But then a classmate was like, 'Oh, you'll never make it through a practice.' Being involved with gymnastics, and then a runner, I was like, 'Okay…I definitely could make it through practice."

She then decided to confide in her parents, who had some reservations.

"My dad kind of was on the edge about it just because I'm a freshman girl going into a high school male dominated sport," she said. "But eventually my mom talked to the coach, and then the coach talked to all the wrestlers, and then my dad was on board, and then I just started."

Felicity Taylor poses in stance. Photo provided by Felicity Taylor.

One positive of being on her team was the support she received from those around her. "We had ten to twelve guys, I think, in my class out (for wrestling). So they all kind of welcomed me really. Because we had some upperclassmen, but most of the team was my classmates. So it was really easy because they all welcomed me and, you know, picked on me, but they're like my brothers. So we just kind of grew closer. The first year was a little rough for me because I wasn't very good. But my support system and the community, my teammates, my coaches, everyone was so good with working with me and supporting me. And I mean, I come home now and they all ask me how college is going. Yeah, I by far have the best support system with coaches, teammates, community. Joining and staying out, it really helps tremendously."

Although she hit the illustrious 100 win mark, she was unsure of the final number. "I'm trying to think. I know I had over 100 wins. I wasn't really big into the record thing because my freshman year was on JV but I think I had like, 10 matches that I won, or 12. I don't really know. I think it was like 103 or 107."

As she accumulated her wins, Taylor remembered wrestling a girl only once.

"I had one against Alaina Sunlin from Monticello. I think that was the only match I had against (a) girl up until Fargo … but during the high school season, I only had one match."

The wrestling team, school, and community rallying behind her was what mattered the most to her. "I just really remember having such a supportive community and teammates. And that really helped me with like I said, staying out and wanting to do better for them. I was the first girl at South Winneshiek to wrestle so it was just kind of new, but everyone accepted it for the most part that I know of."

Her support system was there through the good and the bad.

Having familiar faces all four of the years that Taylor wrestled for South Winneshiek made memories for her. "It was really nice that...my whole team was made up of my classmates, especially my senior year. I still miss it. It was the best year just because I think even my senior year we had like eight guys out in my class. Being able to go throughout the whole high school career with them was awesome."

Felicity Taylor and other girl wrestlers. Photo provided by Felicity Taylor.

She had an important message to pass on to the girls following in her footsteps.

"Just keep going. Sometimes it might be hard, but it's definitely worth it. And high school wrestling might be a bit more difficult because you're wrestling guys and it's not female dominated yet. It's getting there. And they're going to have these opportunities. The more people that stay out, the better it's going to be, so just push through it. If you have a hard time, reach out to someone because we do truly need numbers. And we want these girls out and if they want to be out, they should be. They shouldn't be like, 'Oh, I don't want to wrestle the guys.' They should be having these opportunities. So, for sure, it might be hard, but it's definitely worth it in the end."

2019 IWOCA Girls High School State Meet

On April 14, 2018, the National Association of Intercollegiate Sports, or NAIA, approved women's wrestling as an invitational sport, giving high school girls in Iowa an opportunity to compete in college in the sport they loved.

At the beginning of the 2018-2019 school year, the Iowa High School Athletic Association asked high schools to follow Ogden and Independence's example and add girls divisions to their tournaments. This included Riverside High School in Oakland, City High in Iowa City, Fort Dodge High School in Fort Dodge, Wilton High School in Wilton, Ames High School in Ames, Central Community in Elkader, Ogden High School in Ogden, Thomas Jefferson High School in Council Bluffs, Independence High School in Independence, Ankeny High School in Ankeny, Jefferson High School in Cedar Rapids, and Glenwood High School in Glenwood.

The schedule posted on social media in 2019 to alert girl high school wrestlers of upcoming meets offering all-girls divisions.

Wrestlers who participated in the Wilton girls-only division on December 15, 2018. Photo by Tricia Andersen.

Sydney Park, Ali Andersen, and Rebecca Ferguson at the all-girls division at Ogden High School on December 15, 2018. Photo by Tricia Andersen

Abby McIntyre and Ali Andersen face off in the all-girls division at Ames High School on January 5, 2019. They were the only two to participate that day. Photo by Tricia Andersen.

On January 4, 2019, the IHSAA announced that the Waverly-Shell Rock tournament on January 19th would become the first girls' state wrestling tournament in Iowa history. It would be headed up by the Iowa Wrestling Coaches and Officials Association, or IWOCA. They agreed to be the headline sponsor as well as run the event in conjunction with Waverly-Shell Rock High School.

This tournament was only for those who were girls currently competing on their high school teams. They had to compete in a girls only division to qualify. At the time, 167 girls were wrestling in the Iowa high schools.

However, Iowa winter weather made this event a challenge. A blizzard tore through the state on January 18, leaving it under a blanket of several feet of snow. While over 100 girls had registered for the tournament, only 87 were able to brave the elements to get to Waverly.

The state meet ran in conjunction with Waverly-Shell Rock's JV boys tournament. And despite the foul weather the day before, the stands were packed with fans. After a group picture of the participants was taken, the wrestlers took to the mats to produce the first female state wrestling champions in Iowa high school history.

Ali Gerbracht wrestles Ella Schmit at the IWOCA Iowa Girls High School State Wrestling Meet on. Photo provided by Chad Gerbracht.

The first win of the event was Hannah Michael of Union High School with a pin on Sioux Central's Katy Unger. The first state champion was Ali Gerbracht at 106 pounds. She was accompanied by Tateum Park of Davenport North at 113 pounds, Chloe Clemons of Cedar Rapids Jefferson at 120, Sydney Park of Davenport Central at 126, Annika Behrends of Waverly-Shell Rock at 132, Avery Meier of Waverly-Shell Rock at 138, Toyia Griffin of Nashua-Plainfield at 152, Jacenta Sargisson of LeMars at 170, Millie Peach of Iowa Valley at 195, and Rilee Slycord of Colfax-Mingo at 285.

Chloe Clemon receives her medal at the first IWOCA Iowa Girls High School State Wrestling Meet on January 19, 2019.
Photo by Tricia Andersen.

Waverly-Shell Rock took first as a team, Colfax-Mingo took second, and Charles City took third.

Clemons told KJ Pilcher of The Cedar Rapids Gazette, "It's come a long way since I started back in seventh grade when there really wasn't a whole lot of girls. Being able to have all of us come together in one big tournament, all the brackets and championships, it really is amazing.

"All my practices, all my coaches, all the support and all the technique I learned has really paid off. It's actually unexplainable how amazing it feels."

Millie Peach is hugged by her younger sisters at the IWOCA Iowa Girls High School State Wrestling Meet. Photo by Jeremy Kriegel.

Peach, also interviewed by Pilcher, said, "This is a great opportunity. When I was little they had tiny little (tournaments) and they were all over the place. I would always go to those. Getting to do this in high school and winning is really cool."

Did she see herself as an example for future girl wrestlers in Iowa?

"I hope I am because I have three little sisters who wrestle. By the time the youngest gets up it will probably be an even bigger thing. She's got 10 years to be my age ... Hopefully by then it will be really big and almost as big as the guys' tournament."

The Gazette reported that the IWOCA and others in favor of girls wrestling in Iowa high schools had many talks with the IHSSA and the Iowa Girls High School Athletic Union, or IGHSAU, concerning the sanctioning of girls wrestling.

The discussion was stilted. When the Union was asked what it required to sanction a new sport, the answers were vague. The goals they set would change frequently.

The IWOCA determined to take the step to have the tournament in hopes to propel support towards sanctioning forward.

Bob Murphy, the executive director of the IWOCA, said, "We had some great championship matches. The atmosphere was great and we planned to make it like a regular state tournament.

"I've done a lot of officiating for girls' wrestling and I enjoy it. I think we need to keep pushing and this is just icing on the cake for this year. Hopefully, next year we expand beyond here."

Clemons holds her bracket for photos at the first IWOCA Iowa Girls High School State Wrestling Meet in 2019. Photo by Tricia Andersen.

Clemons chimed in, "That is the ultimate goal for all the girls to wrestle beside the boys and have the big stage and all the amazing people cheering for us. That's what we all hope for."

The Des Moines Register also reported on the event, detailing that only ten weight classes were represented to allow more opportunity for the participants to wrestle. Four brackets had double digit participants, with the largest being 126 at 16 wrestlers. One hundred matches were won by pin during the event.

Sydney Park, the 126 pound state champion, told the Register, "This was amazing. This was a really good first step. Our next step is having more girls' tournaments. It's growing and that's really exciting."

Sydney Park receives her medal at the first IWOCA Iowa Girls High School State Wrestling Meet on January 19, 2019.
Photo by Tricia Andersen.

After winning the 113 state championship and hugging her family who was cheering for her in the stands, her sister Tateum said, "It feels really nice to just have that feeling. My goal has always just to make it to state against the boys, so this opportunity feels amazing."

"I thought this was amazing," Clemens said. "All the girls came together. We had brackets, rankings. It really feels like it's a girls' sport too, not just a boys' sport."

The Register reported some influential guests in attendance at the state meet. Rachel Watters, the first girl to win at sectionals at the higher weight classes during her senior year at Ballard High School in 2016, made the trip to witness the tournament. Jean Berger, the executive director of IGHSAU, also was there to watch the girls make history.

"It warms my heart," Watters said. "I've been sitting in the stands and watching all the girls. There's cheerleaders cheering on the girls. I see the boys' teams in the stands cheering when they win matches.

"This sport is so awesome, and a lot of people are finally on board with giving these girls these opportunities. I think that'll help the movement grow so much faster."

The Waterloo-Cedar Falls Courier interviewed Eric Whitcome, tournament host and head coach of the Waverly-Shell Rock wrestling team, who said about the tournament, "You could say this was kind of thrown together at the last minute, but we got a lot of the right people on board with making it happen. It was a top class event. And most importantly, give credit to the people who deserve it - the girls. A lot of these girls came out over winter break, many of them had never wrestled, but they understood the importance of the movement that was happening and wanted to be part of history being made."

Sydney Park holds her bracket for photos at the first IWOCA Iowa Girls
High School State Wrestling Meet on January 19, 2019.
Photo by Tricia Andersen.

Wrestlers gather for a group photo at the first IWOCA Iowa Girls High School State Wrestling Meet. Photo by Tricia Andersen.

Ali Andersen, Shae Muenke, Sydney Park, and Hannah Michael at the conclusion of the IWOCA Iowa Girls High School State Wrestling MeetPhoto by Tricia Andersen.

Ali Gerbracht wrestles Ella Schmit at the IWOCA Iowa Girls High School
State Wrestling Meet. Photo provided by Chad Gerbracht.

Rylee Slycord on the podium at the IWOCA Iowa Girls High School State
Wrestling Meet. Photo provided by Erin Hume

Colfax-Mingo with their team trophy at the conclusion of the IWOCA Iowa
Girls High School State Wrestling Meet on January 19, 2019. Photo
provided by Erin Hume.

2020 IWOCA Girls High School State Meet

The 2019-2020 girls wrestling season took a dramatic increase from 187 to 559 wrestlers. The girls divisions during the high school season jumped from a handful of competitors to 80-100 per meet.

Ali Andersen, Mariah Webster, and Millie Peach talk together as they wait for their next match during the all-girls division at BGM High School on December 6, 2019. Photo taken by Tricia Andersen.

It began at BGM Brooklyn High School in Brooklyn, Ia, which saw 86 girls in attendance according to TrackWrestling. It was followed by Algona High School in Algona, AP-GC in Parkersburg, Riverside-Oakland in Oakland, Waverly-Shell Rock in Waverly, Des Moines East in Des Moines, City High School in Iowa City, Sergeant Bluff-Luton in Sergeant Bluff, Fort Dodge High School in Fort Dodge, Wilton High School in Wilton, Colfax-Mingo High School in Colfax, Central Community in Elkader, Ogden High School in Ogden, Ames High School in Ames, Logan Magnolia High School in Logan, North Scott High School in Eldridge, LeMars High School in LeMars, Independence, MFL-MarMac High School in Monona, Greene County High School in Jefferson, Glenwood High School in Glenwood, and Atlantic High School in Atlantic.

A group picture of the wrestlers in the all-girls division at BGM High School on December 6, 2019. Photo taken by Tricia Andersen.

Mariah Webster wrestling in the all-girls division at BGM High School on December 6, 2019. Taken by Tricia Andersen.

Millie Peach wrestling in the all-girls division at BGM High School on December 6, 2019. Taken by Tricia Andersen.

Ali Andersen wrestling in the all-girls division at BGM High School on
December 6, 2019. Taken by Tricia Andersen.

Members of the Independence High School girls team during the 2019-2020
season. Photo provided by Matthew Shannon.

Each meet saw dozens of girls competing for their spot at the upcoming state meet at the end of January. In some cases, the large number of girls registering to compete pushed the meet past the capacity it could allow.

In the same fashion, the IWOCA Iowa High School Girls State Tournament on January 24-25, 2020 increased from the 87 female wrestlers who could make it to the tournament to 350. The action started Friday afternoon and spilled over to most of Saturday.

According to the Des Moines Register, six of the eleven weight classes needed 64-person brackets due to the number of wrestlers involved in the tournament. Three more had to be sorted into a 32-person bracket for the same reason. The top two weight classes used 16-person and 8-person brackets.

When the event was over, four wrestlers had repeated their performance from the year before and retained their hold on state titles - Tateum Park (Davenport North) at 113 pounds, Chloe Clemons (Pleasant Valley) at 120 pounds, Sydney Park (Davenport Central) at 120 pounds, and Millie Peach (Iowa Valley) at 195 pounds. They were joined by Ella Schmit of Bettendorf at 106, Glenwood's Abby McIntyre of Glenwood at 132, Janelle Avila of Lisbon at 138, Lakin Lienhard of Crestwood at 145, Alaina Schmidt of Dubuque Wahlert at 152, Kendal Clark of Humboldt at 170, and Salima Omari of Iowa City West at 285.

In duplicate fashion from 2019, Sarah Michael, Hannah Michael's younger sister, picked up the first win of the tournament just like her big sister did the year before.

Waverly-Shell Rock repeated their first place spot as team champions with 156.5 points. Charles City took second with 128 points. First time challengers Dubuque Wahlert placed third with 121 points.

Lienhard, the 145-pound champion, explained to the Waterloo-Cedar Falls Courier that, like many other female wrestlers, wrestling was in her family blood. Her brothers, Chase and Caleb, had competed for Crestwood as well. "I grew up in wrestling, going to tournaments every weekend, so it has been good that I have a wrestling background. It has made it easier."

She also told The Courier about her double sport life. "It is pretty busy. I don't have much time off. Luckily we can practice wrestling in the morning which allows me to focus on basketball in the afternoons."

Warming up before the 2020 IWOCA Girls High School Wrestling Meet.
Photo by Tricia Andersen.

On March 23, 2020, the Des Moines Register announced that the IWOCA Iowa Girls State Wrestling Tournament would relocate from Waverly-Shell Rock High School to the newly built Xtreme Arena in Coralville. It would be held on January 22-23, 2021.

Bob Murphy of the IWOCA said, "The new facilities ... are perfect for this event. We'll be utilizing both Xtream Arena and the GreenState Family Fieldhouse, both state-of-the-art and first-class facilities for our high school athletes."

Taking a group photo before the 2020 IWOCA Girls High School Wrestling Meet. Photo by Tricia Andersen.

Waverly-Shell Rock would partner with two Iowa City high schools, Iowa City High and Iowa City West, to put the event on. Coach Eric Whitcome told the Register, "I'm excited to work with Luke, Josh and their team at Think Iowa City. They know how to put on top notch events like the USAW Olympic Team Trials, 2018 UWW World Cup, and next season's Dan Gable Donnybrook. I know our high school girls will receive the red-carpet treatment."

On January 25, 2020, the NCAA granted women's wrestling an emerging sport status for Division II and Division III with Division I planning to vote in March. However, the rise of COVID-19 delayed the vote until the summer. Finally, on July 17, 2020, Division I also added women's wrestling as an emerging sport.

The Xtream Arena under construction. Photo by Tricia Andersen.

Inside of the Xtream Arena. Photo by Tricia Andersen

Sanctioning Efforts

Despite the rumors of talks about sanctioning girls wrestling after the Centerville Big Red JV tournament in 2017, it has yet to happen. The IGHSAU invited representatives of potential sports to attend one of their meetings in the fall of 2018. According to the Des Moines Register on January 21, 2019, Chloe Clemons attended with her father, James. Those in attendance weren't allowed to endorse their sports. They could only listen to the debate.

However, once the meeting was over, those in support of the potentially added sports were told to voice their opinion to the Union. Hundreds of parents and other advocates of girls wrestling flooded the IGHSAU with emails and letters.

Jason Loyd of Iowa AAU Wrestling and Charlotte Bailey of USA Wrestling drummed up support for the movement both face-to-face with parents and wrestlers and by social media. When the IGHSAU wanted letters from the superintendents of Iowa High Schools expressing their approval of girls wrestling in their schools, Loyd and Bailey encouraged the families they worked with to reach out to their school districts to get their superintendent's backing.

Parents and supporters lobbied their state legislature representatives for help at the governmental level. March of 2020 saw a lull in the movement when the rise of COVID-19 changed priorities for many involved in getting the much needed sanctioning. However, as the 2020-2021 season looms in the near future, the battle for girls wrestling as an official sport on its own in the state of Iowa is picking up steam again.

Kendra Kehrli, a 2013 graduate of East Buchanan High School in Winthrop, Iowa, wrestled for her high school team and is currently the girls wrestling coach.

Explaining what it was like for her as an athlete, she said, "So when I wrestled, I was the only girl in our conference and as far as Des Moines West that I knew my age that wrestled. So I wrestled with our boys, I practiced with all boys. I was fortunate enough to have teammates and coaches that really supported me and were my friends and allies. I know some girls, when I went to college, talk about their past experiences through middle school and elementary and even into high school where they didn't have that. So I was very fortunate enough that I was surrounded by really great people."

She switched gears when she started college to a different martial art competing in Judo at Iowa State for four years, and making the world team there. As she approached graduation, she considered what full-time job suited her.

"But I wasn't done competing," she said.

There weren't many options available for Kehrli to wrestle after high school. "So my options were to go to Kentucky, Canada, California. I'm from Iowa, raised on a farm. I love my family. It would be so hard to move from them. But now looking there's one, Des Moines Grandview. That would have been awesome to have, you know, years ago. But I think it's just awesome that there's so many opportunities now."

Kehrli had to make a determination about her future. "If I could have, I would have gone to a college that also had animal science. Growing up on a farm, that's what I wanted to do. And I thought, you know, if I ever did get hurt, and I chose a college because of wrestling, would I like my future job? So that was really hard. That's when I went to Iowa State and found the Judo club. Judo club is kind of like freestyle and Greco together with more chokes and submissions and armbars. So I found my outlet there."

She decided to wrestle once more and found a college to do that with. "After graduating from Iowa State, I decided that I wasn't done competing and I wanted to get wrestling a go one more time. So I went down to Ottawa, Kansas, to a little small four year private school called Ottawa. And found the women's wrestling team down there, and my coach is actually was from Iran. So he won that Iranian World Championships. And he's super awesome. His name is Mahdi Bigdely and he really took me under his wing. I moved down there by myself, found an apartment, lived down there, did my master's, my MBA. That was a two year program in about 10 months so I fast tracked it. I really enjoyed myself and so now I just want to give back to a sport that gave so much to me."

Now she has come home to coach at the school she began with. "And so, middle school girls this year at East Buchanan, we had four go out. High School, we have one. I'm hoping next year that we can, you know, get five girls out. I think it's just very hard for girls to do something that's not common. They don't have a lot of friends doing it. But just to get one girl there and she brings a friend, and then those two girls bring friends and those girls bring friends, hopefully within five years we have a full team. Yeah, that'd be great."

Being involved as an athlete and now as a coach, she sees the importance of sanctioning girls wrestling. "Sanctioning girls wrestling, I think, is huge. I do see the advantages of the girls who do practice with boys. Biologically and scientifically, boys are stronger than girls when they hit high school and the girls who kind of have to push harder in practice to try to get, you know, score takedown or whatever the technique may be in practice shows in a match that grit that you get where you just kind of are sick of getting pounded on."

She hopes, when sanctioning happens, that it is organized toward the future. "But as far as going into college, we wrestle freestyle. So when girls wrestling does get sanctioned, I do hope at the high school level, it gets sanctioned as freestyle wrestling. It doesn't make sense to me to wrestle folkstyle for four years and learn all the rules and moves, and then having to go to college and learn a whole new point scoring system, all new criteria, advantages, you know. You can tech fall someone in 30 seconds. Two big five point throws. That's cool. But I do think that there is an advantage of learning both folkstyle and freestyle. And I think any college athlete would say the same thing because you have to learn your body's stability differently for each. You know hips are very important in freestyle, but in folkstyle protecting your legs is just as important. I guess it's kind of a different feel for each freestyle and folkstyle."

In September 2020, WIN Magazine interviewed Jean Berger, the executive director of the IGHSAU. She first expressed that she is in support of girls wrestling and is "on their side". She went to the first IWCOA Girls State Meet in 2019 and watched the participation in the 2020 Tournament triple in just a year.

However, WIN Magazine reported that, due to sanctioning procedures and the COVID-19 pandemic, it might take Iowa three more years before they see girls' wrestling sanctioned.

"It is getting there," Berger said. "And maybe it will get there soon."

Unfortunately, the COVID-19 virus did slow the sanctioning movement down. Berger said, "I haven't really heard anything since wrestling season ended. I haven't heard from any other schools who would like to add it in that time. In fairness, wrestling and basketball ended and COVID hit...To be fair, this isn't on anybody's school radar currently."

Before the pandemic hit, the IGHSAU had received 17 letters of commitment of the 50 that are needed for the sanctioning to proceed. Fifteen more had verbally committed to offer their support.

Berger told WIN Magazine, "I've said this before, there are a lot of organizations interested in adding high school wrestling, but I don't know if they are working together. We have four or five different organizations moving in four or five different ways. It would be different if it was one organization moving the sport along. We have parents start to campaign and we get a lot of emails and things and we try to explain this is membership driven. Our member schools have a process to go through if they want to add a new sport."

The IGHSAU laid out the requirements that they must have when a school submits a letter of commitment. The packet has to be less than 30 pages, not including the letter itself, and must include a sample budget outlining financial costs, a proposed time-line for implementation of the sport to interscholastic status in the district, competitive opportunities, facility availability or plans, general competition rules, suggested IGHSAU regulations (playing and practice season, coaching requirements, format for the sport, maximum contests, competition structure), and the signatures of the district school board president, superintendent and the athletics director of the institution.

The IGHSAU was also keeping on mind the health and safety of the sport, growth potential, economic viability of the proposal, and the other sports they were considering.

Berger said, "We kind of approach it from a bigger perspective. What other opportunities are out there for our girls? First from our existing sports, participation in soccer, tennis and golf are growing. I also don't know if we are looking at one particular sport or activity for girls to add. We have heard from rugby, lacrosse and competitive cheer. There are parents besides wrestling parents and schools that have different programs that they would probably like to be considered. I don't know if they are quite as organized or maybe as passionate as wrestling. In Iowa, we know wrestling. It is a lot more familiar to our member schools than lacrosse."

Once the IGHSAU has the 50 letters and reaches 15% of the support required, the proposal to sanction girls wrestling with be taken to the Board of Directors to make the final decision. Berger pointed out that other sports, such as soccer and bowling, took many years to get sanctioned. She also wanted to know whether they would have folkstyle or freestyle wrestling, what officials would be involved, and what would be the breakdown of weight classes.

"There are a lot of people within the communities that have been helpful and very positive and very willing to help move it along and understand the process," Berger said. "They are helping us learn and grow as well. I'm very appreciative of them because I have learned a lot from these folks."

She also stated that there had to be some thought in it. "Early on I heard people say let's just throw a mat down at the boys' state tournament and let the girls wrestle on it. That is not how we run a state championship at the Girls Union. We are about showcasing the talent of the Iowa girl. There are a lot of things we would want to ensure we had in place so that we can continue to move along and move forward with. When I mentioned who will be the officials and who are they, we are not going to be somebody's has-been or some second choice. We don't do it that way. We want our experience to be of a high level and we want to make the right decisions that it ensures that it is so we are not just going to throw a mat down and let them come."

Another advocate for women's wrestling is Coach Dan Gable. Gable, who grew up in Waterloo, Iowa, was undefeated in high school at Waterloo West and suffered only one loss in college. Competing for Iowa State University, he lost his final match during his senior year at the NCAA finals. He won six times at the Midlands Open as well as a gold medal at the 1972 Olympics. He then went on to be the head coach for the University of Iowa Hawkeyes from 1976 to 1997 and led the Hawkeyes to 15 National Championships as well as coached 152 All-Americans, 45 National Champions, 106 Big Ten Champions, and 12 Olympians. He also coached the US Olympic Team three times in 1980, 1984, and 2000.

In late 2020, he was awarded with the Presidential Medal of Freedom, the nation's highest hoor for a civilian.

He told the authors of this book, "In Iowa we have many years of tremendous success in wrestling at all levels. And now with women's wrestling leading the way in adding new programs in the high schools and colleges across the USA it makes perfect sense to keep up with the world development of the sport of female wrestling. I'm looking forward to this advancement within the sport which will help the total sport when done correctly!"

The girls of Iowa who found their place on the wrestling mat have overcome challenges and opposition to be on the mat. While rarely noticed, they managed to achieve many of the same successes as their male counterparts. These female wrestlers have blazed the trail for generations of girls to come. The hope is that, in the near future, they too will have equal representation in high school wrestling in Iowa as a sanctioned sport.

Iowa Girls who wrestled for their High Schools According to TrackWrestling

2013-2014

Taylor Tully	Ballard, IA	126	Fr.
Rachel Watters	Ballard, IA	138	So.
Sydney Moorman	Boone, IA	138	So.
Cassy Herkleman	Cedar Falls, IA	138	Sr.
Hope Luce	Clinton, IA	106	Sr.
Faith Luce	Clinton, IA	120	Sr.
Ellenore Boas	Davis County, IA	126	So.
Didrik Lundtvedt	Decorah, IA	113	So.
Michala Schminkey	Des Moines East, IA	106	So.
Destiny Gonzalez	Des Moines Lincoln, IA	106	Sr.
Sydney Hanrahan	Des Moines Roosevelt, IA	120	Sr.
Anna Poyner	Dike-New Hartford, IA	132	Sr.
Maudi Paniagua	Greene County, IA	132	So.
Tori Goodale	Hudson, IA	106	Jr.
Jasmine Bailey	Iowa City West, IA	106	Sr.
Ariel Hellmann	Laurens-Marathon HS, IA	120	Fr.
Kalleigh Hanson	LeMars, IA	106	Sr.
crystal martin	Mason City, IA	113	So.
Olivia Sunlin	Monticello, IA	106	So.
Madison Petty	Monticello, IA	126	Sr.
Daphne Hoefler	North Cedar, IA	106	Fr.
Cassie Brazelton	Norwalk, IA	106	So.
Amanda Svoboda	Panorama, IA	106	Jr.
Micala Gibson	Pleasant Valley, IA	113	So.
Jorie Trueblood	Prairie Valley, IA	120	Jr.
Soledad Castaneda	Riverside, IA	106	Fr.
Katelyn Donahue	Riverside, IA	126	Sr.
Britany Logsdon	Sioux City East, IA	106	Sr.
Alexas Varela	Sioux City West, IA	113	Jr.
Jackie Mendez	Sioux City West, IA	126	Sr.
Lauren Shipley	South Central Calhoun, IA	106	So.
Alexis Gandara	South Hamilton, IA	106	So.
Hannah Mauritz	Southeast Polk, IA	113	Sr.
Ericka Stoner	Tri-County/Montezuma, IA	152	Fr.
Amela Huskic	Valley , West Des Moines, IA	120	Jr.
Unity Daugherty	Van Buren, IA	106	Sr.
Keysheaa Epps	Waterloo East, IA	113	Fr.
Erica Halferty	Wayne, IA	145	Fr.

2014-2015

Cheyenne Haugen	AGWSR, IA	160	So.
Carolyn Regnas	AHSTW, IA	120	Fr.
Nicole Watters	Ballard, IA	113	Fr.
Taylor Tully	Ballard, IA	132	So.
Rachel Watters	Ballard, IA	145	Jr.
Kaliska Clark	Centerville, IA	106	7th
Ciana Sonberg	Charles City, IA	152	Fr.
Kallie Wilson	Cherokee, Washington, IA	120	Fr.
Faith Leonard	Collins-Maxwell-Baxter, IA	132	Fr.
Tammy Vaughn	Columbus Community, IA	132	Jr.
Cae`Leisheia Wilson-Kurylo	Davenport North, IA	138	Fr.
Jolynn Harris	Des Moines Lincoln, IA	132	Fr.
grace Massier	Des Moines Roosevelt, IA	106	Fr.
keshara james	Des Moines Roosevelt, IA	120	Fr.
amela huskic	Des Moines Roosevelt, IA	152	Sr.
Kali Zufall	Estherville Lincoln Central	195	So.
Mikaela Faught	Forest City, IA	145	Fr.
Erica Stoner	Grinnell, IA	195	So.
Cheyanne Evans	Highland, IA	145	Fr.
Corby Webb	Hudson, IA	113	Fr.
Tori Goodale	Hudson, IA	126	Sr.
JERICA Meana	MFL MARMAC, IA	106	Fr.
Chelbe Feuerhelm	MFL MARMAC, IA	113	Fr.
Adrian Richards	Mount Ayr, IA	113	Sr.
Kristen Young	Newton, IA		So.
Maryann Cutshall	North Butler, IA	170	Fr.
Alanah Vetterick	Norwalk, IA	106	Fr.
McKinna Faulkenberry	OA-BCIG, IA	120	Fr.
Nadia Barajas	Oelwein, IA	132	Jr.
Taelor Bjerke	Pleasantville, IA	120	Fr.
Emily Ries	Regina, IA	106	Jr.
Ana Laura	Regina, IA	120	Jr.
Soledad Castaneda	Riverside, IA	120	So.
Ariel Hellmann	Sioux Central, IA	145	So.
Alexas Varela	Sioux City West, IA	138	Sr.
Makayla Patterson	South Central Calhoun, IA	106	So.
Felicity Taylor	South Winneshiek, IA	106	Fr.
Ysmerai Ek	Storm Lake, IA	126	
Desarae Harris	Waterloo West, IA	170	Jr.
Erica Halferty	Wayne, IA	160	So.

Brittany Shumate	Woodbine, IA	138	Fr.
Christy Nemiela	Woodbine, IA	195	Fr.

2015-2016

Dakota Selby	Albia, IA		126	Fr.
Kylie Siebrecht	Alta-Aurelia, IA	113		So.
Nicole Watters	Ballard, IA		138	So.
Rachel Watters	Ballard, IA		145	Sr.
Chelsea Fishback	Carroll, IA		220	Fr.
Anne Gadient	Cascade, IA		126	So.
Ciana Sonberg	Charles City, IA		145	So.
Tate Hughes	Clarinda, IA		152	Fr.
Dominique Mosier	Clear Creek-Amana, IA		138	Fr.
Tammy Vaughn	Columbus Community, IA		145	Sr.
Brooklyn Taylor	Davenport North, IA		113	So.
Jesse Lo	Denison-Schleswig, IA		145	So.
Jesse Lorano	Denison-Schleswig, IA		145	So.
Jolynn Harris	Des Moines Lincoln, IA		145	So.
Keshara James	Des Moines Roosevelt, IA		120	So.
Grace Massier	Des Moines Roosevelt, IA		120	So.
Tatum Hardman	East Sac County, IA		145	Jr.
Alley Gray	Eddyville-Blakesburg-Fremont		145	Fr.
Kali Zufall	Estherville Lincoln Central		285	Jr.
Courtney Six	Fort Madison, IA		113	Fr.
Maiah Williams	Glenwood, IA		106	Fr.
Aubrey McIntyre	Glenwood, IA		120	Fr.
Erica Stoner	Grinnell, IA		220	Jr.
Margarita Valenzuela	Hampton Dumont, IA		152	Fr.
Corby Webb	Hudson, IA		106	So.
Karleigh Shuff	Indianola, IA		138	Sr.
Jade Charron	Interstate 35, IA		220	Sr.
Lexi Williams	Iowa City West, IA		160	So.
Britany Flockhart	Keokuk, IA		113	Fr.
Jocelyn Hemandez	LeMars, IA		160	Jr.
Samantha Back	Lisbon, IA		132	Fr.
Mercedez Putney	Marshalltown, IA		120	Fr.
Brenna Bohland	MFL MARMAC, IA		106	Fr.
Laura Arroyo-Gaona	Muscatine, IA			Fr.
Emma Cornelison	Nodaway Valley, IA		113	Fr.
Julia Eshelman	Nodaway Valley, IA		145	Fr.
Daphne Hoefler	North Cedar, IA		126	Jr.
Larissa Moore	North Cedar, IA		145	Jr.
Haley Snyder	Northeast Community, IA			So.

Haley Snyder	Northeast Community, IA	182	So.
taylor jorgerson	Northwood-Kensett, IA	145	So.
Alanah Vetterick	Norwalk, IA	120	So.
Mckinna Faulkenberry	OA-BCIG, IA	145	So.
Sadie Durnan	Oelwein, IA	220	Fr.
Chloe Krebsbach	Osage, IA	106	Fr.
Shelby Blake	Osage, IA	113	Fr.
Amaya Graham	Oskaloosa, IA	126	Fr.
Kaia Grham	Oskaloosa, IA	132	Fr.
Morgan Lawson	Ottumwa, IA	106	So.
Kendra Felder	Panorama, IA	120	So.
Kyla Devilbiss	Perry, IA	145	Jr.
Gabriela Castillo	Perry, IA	152	Jr.
Alisha Smith	Pleasant Valley, IA	138	So.
Emily Ries	Regina, Iowa City, IA	106	Sr.
Soledad Castaneda	Riverside. Oakland, IA	126	Jr.
Ariel Hellman	Sheldon/South O'Brien, IA	152	Jr.
J Doe	Shenandoah, IA		Fr.
Brooke Silence	Shenandoah, IA	138	Sr.
Myla Mayo	Sioux City East, IA	113	So.
Makayla Patterson	South Central Calhoun, IA	113	Jr.
Keagan King	South Central Calhoun, IA	120	Fr.
Felicity Taylor	South Winneshiek, IA	113	So.
Rylee Zabac	Starmont, IA	113	Fr.
Melinda Collins	Tipton, IA	195	Jr.
Cheyenne Sedlaecek	WACO, IA	120	Sr.
Erica Halferty	Wayne, IA	182	Jr.
Athena Moad	West Burlington/ Notre Dame/Danville, IA	126	Jr.
Mykenzi Brinkman	Westwood, IA	106	Jr.
Abby Crawford	Westwood, IA	132	Sr.
Kaitlynn Thoreson	Woodbine, IA	126	Fr.
Brittany Shumate	Woodbine, IA	132	So.

2016-2017

Ali Gerbracht	AGWSR, IA	106	Fr.
Sarah True	AHSTW, IA	145	Sr.
Dakotah Selby	Albia, IA	113	So.
Keona Ries	Algona, IA	126	Fr.
Grace Meier	Alta-Aurelia, IA	126	Jr.
Aliya Gurganus	Ames, IA	160	Fr.
Hannah Perkins	Ankeny, IA	113	Fr.
Emma Cockerham	Ankeny, IA	145	Sr.

Corby Webb	Aplington-Parkersburg-GC, IA	113	Jr.
Olivia Dee	Ballard, IA	113	So.
Nicole Watters	Ballard, IA	160	Jr.
Autumn Sharp	Boone, IA	113	Fr.
McKenzee Kempker	Burlington, IA	120	Fr.
Chloey Santee	Cedar Rapids Jefferson, IA	120	So.
Chloe Clemons	Center Point-Urbana, IA	106	Fr.
Ciana Sonberg	Charles City, IA	145	Jr.
Kenzie Shackelford	Clarinda, IA	106	Fr.
Dominique Mosier	Clear Creek-Amana, IA	145	So.
Kennadi Colbert	Clear Lake, IA	126	Fr.
Alyssa Zinke	Clinton, IA	145	Fr.
Mollie Greve	Colfax-Mingo, IA	126	So.
Kyla Lampman	Colfax-Mingo, IA	126	So.
Elizabeth Amigon	Columbus Community, IA	106	Jr.
Liliana Garcia	Davenport Central, IA	170	Sr.
Tateum Park	Davenport North, IA	113	Fr.
Ashley Blackwood	Davenport North, IA	170	Fr.
Jesse Lo	Denison-Schleswig, IA	145	Jr.
Brittany Ferrell-Harris	Des Moines East, IA	120	So.
Aziza Bell	Des Moines East, IA	132	So.
Annatastacia Larpenter	Des Moines Lincoln, IA	113	So.
Chole Pearson	Des Moines Lincoln, IA	120	Fr.
Eh Ku Ku	Des Moines Lincoln, IA	132	Sr.
January Paw	Des Moines Lincoln, IA	132	Sr.
Jolynn Harris	Des Moines Lincoln, IA	138	Jr.
Gabby Swarts	Des Moines North-Hoover	152	So.
Grace Massier	Des Moines Roosevelt, IA	126	Jr.
Emily Thomason	Dike-New Hartford, IA	126	Fr.
Donny Bradburn	Dubuque Hempstead, IA	132	So.
Kali Zufall	Estherville Lincoln Central	220	Sr.
Courtney Six	Fort Madison, IA	113	So.
Julia Smith	Griswold, IA	220	Jr.
Yan Chen	Iowa City City, IA	113	Jr.
Britany Flockhart	Keokuk, IA	113	So.
Shae Muecke	Kingsley-Pierson, IA	106	So.
Rachel Dreeszen	Kingsley-Pierson, IA	220	Sr.
Jocelyn Hernandez	LeMars, IA	152	Sr.
Sheyenne Jochims	Maple Valley-Anthon-Oto Hs	126	Fr.
Alaina Sunlin	Monticello, IA	106	Fr.
Emma Cochran	Moravia, IA	113	So.
Natasha Rojas	Muscatine, IA	126	Fr.
Camrae Schakel	Nevada, IA	132	Fr.

Eden Highland	Nevada, IA	160	Fr.
Shelby Wilke	Northeast Community, IA	182	Jr.
Haley Snyder	Northeast Community, IA	195	Jr.
Annette Casino	Northwood-Kensett, IA	182	So.
Alanah Vetterick	Norwalk, IA	126	Jr.
Chloe Krebsbach	Osage, IA	113	So.
Shelby Blake	Osage, IA	120	So.
Amaya Graham	Oskaloosa, IA	120	So.
Kaia Graham	Oskaloosa, IA	126	So.
Morgan Lawson	Ottumwa, IA	113	Jr.
Alondra Lopez Munoz	Pella, IA		So.
Kyla Devilbiss	Perry, IA	132	Sr.
Zowie Strough	Perry, IA	145	So.
Kimberly Valdez	Perry, IA	182	Jr.
Shelby Lee	Pleasant Valley, IA	132	So.
Alisha Smith	Pleasant Valley, IA	132	Jr.
Alex Chapman	Pleasant Valley, IA	138	Fr.
Gracie Bluml	Riverside. Oakland, IA	106	Fr.
Nayely Martinez	Riverside. Oakland, IA	113	Fr.
Soledad Castaneda	Riverside. Oakland, IA	138	Sr.
Kim Hendrian	Roland-Story, IA	120	Jr.
Leila Seaton	Roland-Story, IA	160	So.
Myla Mayo	Sioux City East, IA	113	Jr.
Allison Aguilar	Sioux City West, IA	138	Fr.
Hannah Payne	South Central Calhoun, IA	113	Fr.
Keagan King	South Central Calhoun, IA	132	So.
Felicity Taylor	South Winneshiek, IA	113	Jr.
Jade Bitting	Southeast Polk, IA	106	So.
Katie Julius	St. Edmond, IA	106	Jr.
Sam Brown	St. Edmond, IA	113	Jr.
Josey Fink	Starmont, IA		Fr.
Teodora Leopold	Starmont, IA	152	Jr.
Sabina Halleman	Tipton, IA	160	Sr.
Hope Johnson	Urbandale, IA	138	So.
Katie Johnson	Waukee, IA	132	Fr.
Matti Pladsen	Waukon, IA	132	Jr.
Sarah Moorman	Wayne, IA	120	Fr.
Erica Halferty	Wayne, IA	170	Sr.
Cailee Henning	West Fork, Sheffield, IA	132	Jr.
Mykenzi Brinkman	Westwood, IA	113	Sr.
Madison Kafton	Westwood, IA	132	So.
Kaitlyn Guy	Woodbine, IA	113	Fr.
Brittney Shumate	Woodbine, IA	132	Jr.

2017-2018

Ali Gerbracht	AGWSR, IA	106	So.
Joselin Baxter	AHSTW, IA	145	
Nola Scherling	Akron-Westfield, IA	145	Fr.
Kalie Gaes	Alta-Aurelia, IA	126	Fr.
Juliana Dias	B-G-M, IA	145	Sr.
Luiza Bianco	B-G-M, IA	182	Sr.
Carolina Cristobal	Boone, IA	285	Fr.
Chloe Clemons	Cedar Rapids Jefferson, IA	120	So.
Alexandra Andersen	Cedar Rapids Kennedy, IA	126	Fr.
Emily Lewis	Centerville, IA	106	Jr.
Shelby Vanderheyden	Centerville, IA	220	Jr.
Evah Owens	Central City, IA	132	Fr.
Emma Cochran	Chariton, IA	106	Jr.
Ashley Gress	Chariton, IA	106	Sr.
Emilee Coates	Chariton, IA	113	So.
Maryim Kopytko	Chariton, IA	138	Sr.
Ciana Sonberg	Charles City, IA	182	Sr.
Kennadi Colbert	Clear Lake, IA	138	So.
Alyssa Zinke	Clinton, IA	152	So.
Mollie Greve	Colfax-Mingo, IA	126	Jr.
Ilia Hostetter	Colfax-Mingo, IA	126	Jr.
Abby Jones	Colfax-Mingo, IA	145	Sr.
Tateum Park	Davenport North, IA	113	So.
Tanaya Turpin	Davenport North, IA	120	Fr.
Hailey Wilkins	Decorah, IA	120	Jr.
Jesse Lo	Denison-Schleswig, IA	145	Sr.
Alexandra Chamu	Des Moines, Abraham Lincoln	106	So.
Chloe Pearson	Des Moines, Abraham Lincoln	120	So.
Jolynn Harris	Des Moines, Abraham Lincoln	132	Sr.
Isabelle Jaimes	Des Moines, Abraham Lincoln	182	So.
Michaela Wagner	Dike-New Hartford, IA	138	Fr.
Lily Bassett	Durant, IA	138	Sr.
K Kennedi Crosby	Eddyville-Blakesburg-Fremont	152	Fr.
Marissa Lacy	Forest City, IA	113	So.
Abby McIntyre	Glenwood, IA	132	Fr.
Jaden Gaylord	Glenwood, IA	195	Fr.
Julia Smith	Griswold, IA	285	Sr.
Carli Ahrenstorff	Hartley-Melvin-Sanborn, IA	113	Sr.
Emily Thomason	Hudson, IA	126	So.
Madison Smith	Indianola, IA	106	Fr.
Sara Elimam	Iowa City West, IA	120	So.

111

Alaa Babekir	Iowa City West, IA	138	Fr.
Shae Muecke	Kingsley-Pierson, IA	106	Jr.
Serenity Stansbury	Kingsley-Pierson, IA	285	Jr.
Olivia Diggins	Logan-Magnolia, IA	132	So.
Maddy Buffum	Logan-Magnolia, IA	138	Fr.
Kaylei Ilai	Maquoketa, IA	106	So.
Trisda Capelle	Maquoketa, IA	138	Fr.
Emlie Smith-Mess	Marion, IA	152	Jr.
McKenna Wohlers	Missouri Valley, IA	132	Sr.
Hope Hunter	Monticello, IA	106	Fr.
Alaina Sunlin	Monticello, IA	113	So.
Madeline Kelley	Moravia, IA	113	Sr.
Emma Faust	Muscatine, IA	106	So.
Camrae Schakel	Nevada, IA	145	So.
Kiara Musser	North Cedar, IA	120	Jr.
schelby wilke	Northeast Community, IA		Sr.
shelby wilke	Northeast Community, IA	195	Sr.
haley snyder	Northeast Community, IA	220	Sr.
Jasmine Mueggenberg	Norwalk, IA	132	Fr.
Chloe Krebsbach	Osage, IA	113	Jr.
Kate Mostek	Osage, IA	126	Jr.
Kaia Graham	Oskaloosa, IA	138	Jr.
Jade Davis	Ottumwa, IA	113	Fr.
Mya Davis	Ottumwa, IA	120	Fr.
Morgan Lawson	Ottumwa, IA	120	Sr.
Hannah Jeffrey	Ottumwa, IA	152	Sr.
Sabrina Morrow	Ottumwa, IA	195	So.
Alisha Smith	Pleasant Valley, IA	138	Sr.
Alex Champman	Pleasant Valley, IA	152	So.
Carrie Turner	Postville, IA	145	Sr.
Kim Hendrian	Roland-Story, IA	132	Sr.
Hannah Cree	Roland-Story, IA	145	Fr.
Myla Mayo	Sioux City East, IA	106	Sr.
Sky Smith	Sioux City East, IA	138	Sr.
Luz Villegas	Sioux City West, IA	145	Fr.
Hannah Payne	South Central Calhoun, IA	120	So.
Keagan King	South Central Calhoun, IA	132	Jr.
Leila Seaton	South Hamilton, IA	152	Jr.
Sharlie Waseskuk	South Tama County, IA	126	Jr.
Felicity Taylor	South Winneshiek, IA	113	Sr.
Jade Bitting	Southeast Polk, IA	113	Jr.
Kari German	Starmont, IA	120	So.
Hannah Michael	Union, IA	106	Jr.

Kennedy Lawrence	Valley, West Des Moines, IA	182	Fr.
Jayden Bentley	Waterloo East, IA	160	Fr.
Bianca Macias	Waukee, IA	182	Fr.
Matti Pladsen	Waukon, IA	138	Sr.
Sarah Moorman	Wayne, IA	145	So.
Alexis Partida	West Liberty, IA	113	So.
Bella Roads	Williamsburg, IA	113	Sr.
Kaitlyn Guy	Woodbine, IA	113	So.
Audrey Ireland	Woodbine, IA	126	Fr.
Brittney Shumate	Woodbine, IA	126	Sr.

2018-2019

Ali Gerbracht	AGWSR, IA	106	Jr.
Allison Baxter	AHSTW, IA	145	Fr.
Alia Gale	Benton Community, IA	145	So.
Ella Schmit	Bettendorf, IA	106	Fr.
Anna Sondall	Boone, IA	120	Fr.
Zoey Rice	Carlisle, IA	126	So.
Ella Smith	Cedar Falls, IA	132	Fr.
Jacey Archibald	Cedar Rapids Jefferson, IA	106	Jr.
Chloe Clemons	Cedar Rapids Jefferson, IA	126	Jr.
Gabby Guenther	Cedar Rapids Jefferson, IA	126	Fr.
Karmen Hawkins	Cedar Rapids Jefferson, IA	132	Fr.
Tionne Williams	Cedar Rapids Jefferson, IA	285	Fr.
Alexandra Andersen	Cedar Rapids Kennedy, IA	126	So.
Joslyn DeBurkarte	Cedar Rapids Washington	145	Jr.
Blake DeSilva	Cedar Rapids Washington	195	Jr.
Emily Lewis	Centerville, IA	106	Sr.
Adrianna Kossuthova	Centerville, IA	113	So.
Shelby Vanderheyden	Centerville, IA	195	Sr.
Evah Owens	Central City, IA	138	So.
Emma Cochran	Chariton, IA	113	Sr.
Ashlynn Cother	Charles City, IA		So.
Marissa Bengston	Charles City, IA	113	So.
Toni Maloy	Charles City, IA	126	So.
Emma Grimm	Charles City, IA	132	So.
Marley Hagarty	Charles City, IA	132	So.
Emma Perez	Charles City, IA	132	So.
Allie Cross	Charles City, IA	145	So.
Sydney Peterson	Charles City, IA	195	So.
Kalysta Rodriguez	Charles City, IA	285	Jr.
Jessica Guerrero	Clarke, IA	132	Fr.
Metzli Yanez	Clarke, IA	145	Fr.

Joana Tomas Francisco	Clarke, IA	152	Fr.
Michaela Blume	Clayton Ridge, IA	132	So.
Kennadi Colbert	Clear Lake, IA	138	Jr.
Grace Beard	Clear Lake, IA	145	Jr.
Alyssa Zinke	Clinton, IA	152	Jr.
Ilia Hostetter	Colfax-Mingo, IA	120	Sr.
Kylie Doty	Colfax-Mingo, IA	132	Fr.
Kyla Lampman	Colfax-Mingo, IA	132	Sr.
Mariah Webster	Colfax-Mingo, IA	132	Fr.
Samantha Pierce	Colfax-Mingo, IA	170	Fr.
Chloe Forck	Colfax-Mingo, IA	182	Jr.
Destiny McBride-Dannels	Colfax-Mingo, IA	220	Fr.
Jaycie Webster	Colfax-Mingo, IA	220	Sr.
Rilee Slycord	Colfax-Mingo, IA	285	Sr.
Hannah Raney	Council Bluffs Abraham Lincoln	120	Fr.
Linda Amador	Council Bluffs Thomas Jefferson	120	Fr.
Sydney Park	Davenport Central, IA	126	Fr.
Tateum Park	Davenport North, IA	113	Jr.
Tanaya Turpin	Davenport North, IA	126	So.
Evelyn Henschen	Denison-Schleswig, IA	145	Jr.
Grace Beck	Denver, IA	106	Jr.
Grace Lyons	Denver, IA	106	Fr.
Natalee Lyons	Denver, IA		
Ireland Pollock	Denver, IA	120	So.
Emily Ruby	Denver, IA	120	So.
Elle Block	Denver, IA	126	Jr.
Olivia Decker	Denver, IA	126	So.
Jess Moore	Denver, IA	126	Fr.
Allison Waterman	Denver, IA	132	Sr.
Jaci Carter	Denver, IA	138	Sr.
Cylee Liddle	Denver, IA	138	So.
Gabby Corday	Denver, IA	145	Sr.
Bella Laures	Denver, IA	145	Jr.
Hailey Knoll	Denver, IA	152	Jr.
Brittany Shover	Denver, IA	152	Jr.
Cassie Rizer	Denver, IA	160	Jr.
Lila Meyer	Denver, IA	170	Sr.
AJ Hicks	Des Moines Abraham Lincoln		So.
Deyauna Kinney	Des Moines East, IA	152	
Olivia mulford	Des Moines Roosevelt, IA	120	Fr.
eeden highland	Des Moines Roosevelt, IA	160	Jr.
Elizabeth Wurzer	Durant, IA		Sr.
Brooke Ransford	Eddyville-Blakesburg-Fremont	152	Fr.

Nevaeh Briggs	English Valleys-Tri County, IA	138	Fr.
Teya Ebert	Fairfield, IA	152	Fr.
Kelsy Siddell	Forest City, IA	182	Jr.
Abby McIntyre	Glenwood, IA	132	So.
Jaden Gaylord	Glenwood, IA	220	So.
Madison Petersen	Graettinger-Terril/ Ruthven-Ayrshire, IA	126	Jr.
Karley Havener	Hinton, IA	113	Fr.
Madison Goosmann	Hinton, IA	152	Fr.
Sara Elimam	Iowa City, Liberty, IA	120	Jr.
Emma Barker	Iowa City, Liberty, IA	132	Fr.
Haley Grahlman-Matheny	Iowa City, Liberty, IA	160	Jr.
Millie Peach	Iowa Valley, IA	195	So.
Shae Muecke	Kingsley-Pierson, IA	113	Sr.
Serenity Rex	Kingsley-Pierson, IA	182	Fr.
Jaycee Davison	LeMars, IA	120	So.
Josie Matgen	LeMars, IA	170	So.
Jacenta Sargisson	LeMars, IA	170	Jr.
Claire Ohlrichs	LeMars, IA	195	Sr.
Olivia Diggins	Logan-Magnolia, IA	138	Jr.
Reanna Rife	Logan-Magnolia, IA	145	Jr.
Jade Armbruster	Maquoketa, IA	106	Jr.
Shyanne Valladares	Marshalltown, IA	132	Fr.
Rylee Vercande	Mid-Prairie, IA	132	Fr.
Halle Coenen	Missouri Valley, IA	106	Fr.
Haley Bowman	Missouri Valley, IA	126	Fr.
Madison Buffum	Missouri Valley, IA	145	So.
Alaina Sunlin	Monticello, IA		Jr.
Hope Hunter	Monticello, IA	106	So.
Abby Blint	Mount Pleasant, IA	106	Fr.
Virginia Cacho	Muscatine, IA	120	So.
jasmyn jost	Nashua-Plainfield, IA	113	Fr.
toyia griffin	Nashua-Plainfield, IA	152	So.
Camrae Schakel	Nevada, IA	145	Jr.
Lourdes Underberg	Newton, IA		Sr.
Sophia Adams	NH/TV, IA	126	So.
Ashlynn Miller	North Cedar, IA	120	Fr.
Eve Yezek	Northwood-Kensett, IA	120	Jr.
TeAnna Ausborn	Northwood-Kensett, IA	138	Fr.
Juana Jones	Notre Dame, Burlington, IA	145	Fr.
Lauren Hamilton	Oelwein, IA	113	Fr.
Falynn Buehler	Oelwein, IA	120	Fr.
Carley Jeanes	Oelwein, IA	120	Sr.

Morgan Alber	Oelwein, IA	126	Fr.
Liz Reinhart	Oelwein, IA	132	Jr.
Naomi Gaede	Oelwein, IA	138	So.
Dayna Van DeWalker	Oelwein, IA	145	Jr.
Jordan Lammers	Oelwein, IA	152	Sr.
Torianne Ausmus	Oelwein, IA	285	Sr.
Chloe Krebsbach	Osage, IA	106	Sr.
Karlie Wagner	Osage, IA	106	So.
Madison Adams	Osage, IA	120	Jr.
Sadie Clayton	Osage, IA	126	Sr.
Katelyn Halbach	Osage, IA	126	Sr.
Clarissa Huisman	Osage, IA	126	Jr.
Kate Mostek	Osage, IA	126	Sr.
Madison Brown	Osage, IA	132	So.
Maegan Krebsbach	Osage, IA	132	Fr.
Ashlynn Brock	Osage, IA	138	Jr.
Lauren Voaklander	Osage, IA	138	Jr.
Makayla Mostek	Osage, IA	145	Jr.
MercedeRose Wiese	Osage, IA	145	So.
Jade Davis	Ottumwa, IA		So.
Hannah Jeffrey	Ottumwa, IA		Fr.
Morgan Lawson	Ottumwa, IA		Fr.
Sabrina Morrow	Ottumwa, IA		Jr.
Madeline Black	Pekin, IA	106	Fr.
Phoebe Huber	Pekin, IA	152	Fr.
Aine Moffit	Pleasant Valley, IA	145	Fr.
Sayde Mull	Pleasantville, IA	113	Jr.
Brynn Miller	Pleasantville, IA	120	Fr.
Emma Wall	Prairie, Cedar Rapids, IA	113	Fr.
Karen Meyer	Ridge View, IA	170	Fr.
Nayely Martinez	Riverside, Oakland, IA	106	So.
Iliana Yanes	Riverside, Oakland, IA	285	So.
Katy Unger	Sioux Central, IA	113	Jr.
Dannie Richardson	Sioux Central, IA	138	So.
Morgan Griffin	Sioux Central, IA	170	Fr.
Yareli Morales	Sioux City East, IA	120	Fr.
Kada Webb	Sioux City West, IA	120	So.
Hannah Payne	South Central Calhoun, IA	120	Jr.
Keagan King	South Central Calhoun, IA	126	Sr.
Leila Seaton	South Hamilton, IA	182	Sr.
Marisol Mora	South Tama County, IA	106	Sr.
Ashton Graham	South Tama County, IA	138	Sr.
Tyra Joy	South Tama County, IA	145	Sr.

Sierra Saufley	Southwest Iowa, IA	120	Sr.
Kennedy Lamkins	Southwest Iowa, IA	138	So.
Hailie Vlaminck	Spencer, IA	145	Fr.
Lexi Duong	St. Albert, IA	126	Sr.
Elly Berry	St. Edmond, IA	113	Fr.
Kari German	Starmont, IA	113	Jr.
Hannah Michael	Union, IA	106	Sr.
Jazmyn Knutson	Valley, West Des Moines, IA	132	Fr.
Saida Komjo	Valley, West Des Moines, IA	145	Fr.
Kennedy Lawrence	Valley, West Des Moines, IA	160	So.
Jayden Bentley	Waterloo East, IA	160	So.
Kiara MccGee	Waterloo East, IA	160	So.
Carlie Frost	Waterloo West, IA	145	Sr.
Riley Rodish	Waukee, IA	113	Fr.
Meridian Snitker	Waukon, IA	120	Fr.
Regan Griffith	Waukon, IA	126	So.
Nevaeh Bushaw	Waukon, IA	182	So.
Rose Giesler	Waverly-Shell Rock, IA	120	Sr.
Cailey Reyna	Waverly-Shell Rock, IA	126	Jr.
Jacey Meier	Waverly-Shell Rock, IA	132	Sr.
Abby Bechtel	Waverly-Shell Rock, IA	138	Sr.
Annika Behrends	Waverly-Shell Rock, IA	138	Fr.
Grace Golly	Waverly-Shell Rock, IA	138	So.
Avery Meier	Waverly-Shell Rock, IA	138	So.
Rachel Roose	Waverly-Shell Rock, IA	145	Jr.
Haley Eckerman	Waverly-Shell Rock, IA	152	Jr.
Hedda Kveum	Waverly-Shell Rock, IA	152	Sr.
Hanna Johnson	Waverly-Shell Rock, IA	182	Sr.
Sarah Moorman	Wayne, IA	132	Jr.
Emma Johnson	West Central Valley, IA	132	So.
Alexis Partida	West Liberty, IA	106	Jr.
Mylei Henderson	West Liberty, IA	145	Fr.
Summer Landen-Allen	West Lyon, IA	106	So.
Zoe Barrett	Wilton, IA	138	So.
Mea Burkle	Wilton, IA	138	So.
Oakley Van Pelt	Woodbine, IA	126	Fr.
Kaitlyn Guy	Woodbine, IA	132	Jr.
Audrey Ireland	Woodbine, IA	138	So.

2019-2020

Denyla Wells	ADM, IA	182	Fr.
Taryn Day	AGWSR, IA	132	Fr.

Trinity Rotgers	AGWSR, IA	138	Fr.
Ali Gerbracht	AGWSR, IA	106	Sr.
Bella Canada	AHSTW, IA	170	Fr.
Allison Baxter	AHSTW, IA	160	So.
Serenity Kinter	Algona, IA	106	Fr.
Eliza Schultz	Algona, IA	120	Fr.
Caitlin Shannon	Algona, IA	138	Fr.
Kylie Barnett	Algona, IA	170	Fr.
Radaisyia Thomas	Algona, IA	120	So.
Kaylee Cook	Algona, IA	145	So.
Sophie Degner	Algona, IA	152	So.
Madi Gifford	Algona, IA	160	So.
Alasha Heenan	Algona, IA	170	So.
Willow Kent	Algona, IA	220	So.
Bethany Carlson	Algona, IA	145	Jr.
Brooklynn Wille	Algona, IA	126	Sr.
Sydney Hoover	Algona, IA	145	Sr.
Autumn Perry	Algona, IA	195	Sr.
Maddie McPeak	Algona, IA	220	Sr.
Savannah Williams	Ames, IA	132	Fr.
Linda Green	Ames, IA	138	Fr.
Maggie Wagner	Anamosa, IA	120	Fr.
Ava Scranton	Anamosa, IA	126	Fr.
Emily Waters	Anamosa, IA	126	Fr.
Mya Ludwig	Anamosa, IA	138	Fr.
Bri Neuhaus	Anamosa, IA	138	Fr.
Katie Murdock	Anamosa, IA	126	So.
Grace Titter	Anamosa, IA	220	So.
Starr Kirk	Anamosa, IA	120	Jr.
Keali Koppes	Anamosa, IA	120	Jr.
Jasmine Jacobson	Anamosa, IA	126	Jr.
Chloe Kannaberg	Anamosa, IA	132	Jr.
Haven Baker	Anamosa, IA	138	Jr.
Kyla Callaway	Anamosa, IA	170	Jr.
Jordan Erikson	Anamosa, IA	145	Sr.
Serina Norte	Anamosa, IA	145	Sr.
Avery Grim	Ankeny Centennial, IA	132	Fr.
Olivia Foddrill	Ankeny Centennial, IA	106	So.

Grace Gray	Ankeny Centennial, IA	220	So.
Isabella Dietrich	Ankeny Centennial, IA	113	Sr.
Sophie Lee	Ankeny Centennial, IA	126	Sr.
Jones Marissa	Ankeny Centennial, IA	138	Sr.
Lauren Oliver	Ankeny Centennial, IA	138	Sr.
Lexie Magner	Ankeny Centennial, IA	152	Sr.
Grace Coates	AP-GC, IA	138	Sr.
Kenzie Hoffman	Atlantic-CAM, IA	160	So.
Lexie Trotter	Atlantic-CAM, IA	182	So.
Aleigh Bean	Atlantic-CAM, IA	126	Sr.
Kayla Mauk	Atlantic-CAM, IA	145	Sr.
Maddy Fell	Atlantic-CAM, IA	152	Sr.
Liberty Tupper	BCLUW-SH, IA	120	Fr.
Brianna Griffth	Belle Plaine, IA	132	So.
Joslyn Bordwell	Belmond-Klemme, IA	145	Fr.
Taylor Nelson	Belmond-Klemme, IA	106	Sr.
Lauren Rogalla	Bettendorf, IA	106	Fr.
Ella Schmit	Bettendorf, IA	106	So.
Chloe Etten	BGM, Brooklyn, IA	145	Fr.
Jessica Haines	BGM, Brooklyn, IA	145	Fr.
Anna Sondall	Boone, IA	126	So.
Lauren Snyder	Cardinal Community, IA	106	Jr.
Kenedi Keesey	Carlisle, IA	120	Jr.
Zoe Rice	Carlisle, IA	126	Jr.
Jessica Doss	Carlisle, IA	160	Sr.
Raelynn Strelow	Cedar Falls, IA	113	So.
Ella Smith	Cedar Falls, IA	138	So.
Josie Klemke	Cedar Falls, IA	152	Jr.
Raelynn Smith	Cedar Falls, IA	113	Sr.
Abbie Lyman	Cedar Falls, IA	120	Sr.
Nadia Garcia-Santiago	Cedar Rapids Jefferson, IA	132	Fr.
Solange Kafunda	Cedar Rapids Jefferson, IA	120	So.
Gabby Guenther	Cedar Rapids Jefferson, IA	132	So.
Karmen Hawkins	Cedar Rapids Jefferson, IA	132	So.
Lexi Mikulas	Cedar Rapids Jefferson, IA	220	Jr.
Skyler Lynas	Cedar Rapids Jefferson, IA	138	Sr.
Crystal Talley	Cedar Rapids Jefferson, IA	138	Sr.
Evann Biedenbach	Cedar Rapids Jefferson, IA	145	Sr.

Katherine Hodel	Cedar Rapids Jefferson, IA	145	Sr.
Alyssa Smith	Cedar Rapids Jefferson, IA	145	Sr.
Alexandra Andersen	Cedar Rapids Kennedy, IA	126	Jr.
Joslyn DeBurkarte	Cedar Rapids Washington, IA	132	Sr.
Moorea Brown	Center Point-Urbana, IA	138	Fr.
Sarah Lewis	Centerville, IA	132	Fr.
Caca Oliveira	Centerville, IA	152	Jr.
Evah Owens	Central City, IA	138	Jr.
Rebecca Suhr	Central Community, Elkader, IA	160	Fr.
Claire Thiese	Central Community, Elkader, IA	160	Fr.
Brittni Tieden	Central Community, Elkader, IA	120	Jr.
Maria Medberry	Central Community, Elkader, IA	132	Jr.
Jasmine Mueller	Central Community, Elkader, IA	132	Sr.
Riley Sellergren	Central Springs, IA	106	Sr.
Haddon Anderson	Chariton, IA	106	Fr.
Alexis Alexander	Chariton, IA	113	Fr.
Alena Rudenko	Chariton, IA	120	Fr.
Joslyn Smith	Chariton, IA	160	Fr.
Vivian Bauer	Chariton, IA	106	So.
Brisa Rivera	Chariton, IA	113	Jr.
Tiffany Kern	Chariton, IA	152	Sr.
Elizabeth Oleson	Charles City, IA	113	Fr.
Kaylin Patten	Charles City, IA	120	Fr.
Lilly Luft	Charles City, IA	132	Fr.
Morgan Maloy	Charles City, IA	138	Fr.
Tatiana Bowdery	Charles City, IA	285	Fr.
Sydney Peterson	Charles City, IA		Jr.
Marissa Gallup	Charles City, IA	106	Jr.
Kiki Connell	Charles City, IA	120	Jr.
Emma Perez	Charles City, IA	120	Jr.
Toni Maloy	Charles City, IA	126	Jr.
Allie Cross	Charles City, IA	145	Jr.
Lauren Connell	Charles City, IA	170	Sr.
Kalysta Rodriguez	Charles City, IA	285	Sr.
Jessica Guerrero	Clarke, Osceola/Murray, IA	126	So.
Metzli Yanez	Clarke, Osceola/Murray, IA	145	So.
Michaela Blume	Clayton Ridge, IA	132	Jr.
Bela Upchurch	Clear Creek-Amana, IA	145	So.

Kennadi Colbert	Clear Lake, IA	132	Sr.
Sydney Burlingame	Clinton, IA	138	Fr.
Emmalee Goldensoph	Clinton, IA	195	Fr.
Judith Goetz	Colfax-Mingo, IA	106	Fr.
Addi Mayes	Colfax-Mingo, IA	120	Fr.
Samantha Haney	Colfax-Mingo, IA	126	Fr.
Danica Linn	Colfax-Mingo, IA	120	So.
Kylie Doty	Colfax-Mingo, IA	132	So.
Mariah Webster	Colfax-Mingo, IA	132	So.
Kirsten Frier	Colfax-Mingo, IA	138	So.
Maggie Schroeder	Colfax-Mingo, IA	160	So.
Samantha Pierce	Colfax-Mingo, IA	195	So.
Katie Schlosser	Colfax-Mingo, IA	195	So.
Destiny McBride-Dannels	Colfax-Mingo, IA	220	So.
Riley Carrol	Colfax-Mingo, IA	132	Jr.
Elayna Creech	Colfax-Mingo, IA	145	Jr.
Miranda McGill	Colfax-Mingo, IA	152	Jr.
Nicolasa Hernandez	Colfax-Mingo, IA	126	Sr.
Abigail Dille	Colfax-Mingo, IA	132	Sr.
Chloe Forck	Colfax-Mingo, IA	182	Sr.
Avery Wilson	Colfax-Mingo, IA	285	Sr.
Jaqueline Bunten	Council Bluffs Abraham Lincoln	138	Fr.
Hannah Davis	Council Bluffs Abraham Lincoln	113	So.
Mallory Hoogestraat	Council Bluffs Thomas Jefferson	182	So.
Rodnesia Smith-Carter	Council Bluffs Thomas Jefferson	126	Sr.
Sierra Hansmeier	Crestwood, Cresco, IA	120	Fr.
Alysa Kennedy	Crestwood, Cresco, IA	120	Fr.
Saydey Scholbrock	Crestwood, Cresco, IA	160	Fr.
jacy kriener	Crestwood, Cresco, IA	120	So.
Berlin Nibblelink	Crestwood, Cresco, IA	126	So.
Sadie Omar	Crestwood, Cresco, IA	126	So.
Emily Voyna	Crestwood, Cresco, IA	126	So.
Marissa Bronner	Crestwood, Cresco, IA	132	So.
Brylee Ruppert	Crestwood, Cresco, IA	160	So.
Lexi Hoppe	Crestwood, Cresco, IA	120	Jr.
Ashley Ferrie	Crestwood, Cresco, IA	126	Jr.
Amanda Lievano	Crestwood, Cresco, IA	145	Jr.
Morgan Moser	Crestwood, Cresco, IA	145	Jr.

Lauren Trende	Crestwood, Cresco, IA	145	Jr.
Annamae Leverson	Crestwood, Cresco, IA	182	Jr.
Chloe Rice	Crestwood, Cresco, IA	132	Sr.
Krista Riley	Crestwood, Cresco, IA	132	Sr.
Lakin Lienhard	Crestwood, Cresco, IA	145	Sr.
Olivia Hamma	Davenport Central, IA	120	Fr.
Sydney Park	Davenport Central, IA	126	So.
Tateum Park	Davenport North, IA	113	Sr.
Jocelyn Cox	Davis County, IA	120	Fr.
Ella Grouws	Decorah, IA		Fr.
Ashley Bjork	Decorah, IA	106	Fr.
Rorie Wiedow	Decorah, IA	113	Fr.
Dahlyn Headington	Decorah, IA	120	Fr.
Mairi Sessions	Decorah, IA	138	Fr.
Rebekah Pedlar	Decorah, IA	145	Fr.
Anya Lovstuen	Decorah, IA	120	So.
Kaia Neal	Decorah, IA	126	Jr.
Isabel Ihde	Decorah, IA	132	Jr.
Jane Murphy	Decorah, IA	170	Jr.
Meg Sessions	Decorah, IA	152	Sr.
Payton Schutte	Decorah, IA	170	Sr.
Chevelle Gefaller	Denver, IA	113	Fr.
Emma Thurm	Denver, IA	132	Fr.
Lauren Nicholas	Denver, IA	152	Fr.
Jada Meier	Denver, IA	106	So.
Jess Moore	Denver, IA	120	So.
Emily Ruby	Denver, IA	126	Jr.
Jayden Bahlmann	Denver, IA	132	Jr.
Morgan Smith	Denver, IA	182	Jr.
Hailey Knoll	Denver, IA	138	Sr.
Brittany Shover	Denver, IA	138	Sr.
Cassie Rizer	Denver, IA	160	Sr.
Marissa Leisinger	Denver, IA	285	Sr.
Serenity White	Des Moines East, IA		Fr.
Kayte Yaw	Des Moines East, IA	182	Fr.
Portia Jones	Des Moines East, IA		Jr.
Alena Maylone	Des Moines North-Hoover, IA		So.
Mia Muhammad	Des Moines Roosevelt, IA	170	Fr.

Carley Hafel	Dubuque Senior, IA		Fr.
Hannah Reel	Dubuque Senior, IA	126	Fr.
Meara Neuwoehner	Dubuque Senior, IA	138	Fr.
Marissa Kamm	Dubuque Senior, IA	160	Fr.
Kes Whalen	Dubuque Senior, IA	145	Sr.
Carlie Jo Fusco	Durant, IA	113	Fr.
Ellie Fuller-Long	Durant, IA	132	So.
Ashley Ramirez	Eagle Grove, IA	160	So.
Keeley Kehrli	East Buchanan, IA	160	Fr.
Mireya Vasquez	East Marshall/GMG, IA	152	Fr.
Kiersten Carroll	East Sac County, IA	113	Fr.
Olivia Villegas	East Sac County, IA	126	Fr.
Chloe Cornelius	East Sac County, IA	152	Fr.
Megan Ingersoll	East Sac County, IA	120	Jr.
Laryn Sharp	East Sac County, IA	145	Jr.
Maddie Black	Eddyville-Blakesburg-Fremont, IA	106	So.
Nevaeh Bushaw	Edgewood-Colesburg, IA	160	Jr.
Nevaeh Briggs	English Valleys-Tri County, IA	132	So.
Zaelynn Downing	English Valleys-Tri County, IA	152	So.
Megan Sautter	Epworth, Western Dubuque, IA	126	Fr.
Keisha Walker	Epworth, Western Dubuque, IA	145	Fr.
Josie Jecklin	Epworth, Western Dubuque, IA	152	Fr.
Mya Lindauer	Epworth, Western Dubuque, IA	152	Fr.
Peyton McCabe	Fairfield, IA	113	Fr.
Teya Ebert	Fairfield, IA	170	So.
Alexis Ross	Fort Dodge, IA	138	Fr.
Abby McIntyre	Glenwood, IA	132	Jr.
Emma Halterman	Greene County, IA	132	Fr.
Emma Hoyle	Greene County, IA	145	Fr.
Aundraya Hernandez	Grinnell, IA	138	Fr.
Maddie Peiffer	Highland, Riverside, IA	138	So.
Kali Beaman	Humboldt, IA	138	Fr.
Ashlyn Sutterfield	Humboldt, IA	106	So.
Baylie Beers	Humboldt, IA	126	So.
Maria Elizond	Humboldt, IA	170	So.
Abby Saturn	Humboldt, IA	113	Jr.
Breanna Hotevec	Humboldt, IA	120	Jr.
Deni McDaniel	Humboldt, IA	138	Jr.

Yuli Orona	Humboldt, IA	145	Jr.
Alexa Hemmelrick	Humboldt, IA	152	Jr.
Emily Zaugg	Humboldt, IA	152	Jr.
Kendal Clark	Humboldt, IA	170	Jr.
Kirstyn Beaman	Humboldt, IA	132	Sr.
Tristan Filler	Humboldt, IA	132	Sr.
Mady Lange	Humboldt, IA	138	Sr.
Hannah Muir	Humboldt, IA	160	Sr.
Tia Woeste	Humboldt, IA	195	Sr.
Chevelle Hookom	Independence, IA	120	Fr.
Dakota Whitman	Independence, IA	120	Fr.
Katelyn VanBuren	Independence, IA	132	Fr.
Rachel Eddy	Independence, IA	182	Fr.
Layla Walker	Independence, IA	182	Fr.
Natalee Anderson	Independence, IA	138	So.
Melody Kremer	Independence, IA	138	So.
Khyley McGrath	Independence, IA	160	So.
Lillian Henkes	Independence, IA	145	Sr.
Kenzie Fischels	Independence, IA	170	Sr.
Alazaya Whitten	Indianola, IA	113	Fr.
Emily Jones	Indianola, IA	126	Fr.
Josephine Wearmouth	Interstate 35, IA	132	So.
Sara Elimam	Iowa City, City High, IA	132	Sr.
Khairah Wright	Iowa City, West, IA	113	Fr.
Amelia Stevens	Iowa City, West, IA	120	Fr.
Alexis Mapel	Iowa City, West, IA	126	Fr.
Eva Jordan	Iowa City, West, IA	132	Fr.
Howaida Musa	Iowa City, West, IA	152	Fr.
Emily Elizadale	Iowa City, West, IA	170	Fr.
Marissa Goodale	Iowa City, West, IA	106	So.
Rawan Guzouli	Iowa City, West, IA	120	So.
Florence Assumani	Iowa City, West, IA	126	So.
Tremeice Carter	Iowa City, West, IA	126	So.
Ava Davis	Iowa City, West, IA	126	So.
Miranda Feng	Iowa City, West, IA	126	So.
Celestina Nuro-Gyina	Iowa City, West, IA	126	So.
Emma Dunlap	Iowa City, West, IA	132	So.
Mattie Harms	Iowa City, West, IA	138	So.

Emma Barker	Iowa City, West, IA	152	So.
Maddie Caylor	Iowa City, West, IA	160	So.
Mayowa Dokun	Iowa City, West, IA	160	So.
Nikki Pinter	Iowa City, West, IA	182	So.
Rhiannon Uetz	Iowa City, West, IA	195	So.
Katie Hoefer	Iowa City, West, IA	126	Jr.
Sophia Strathearn	Iowa City, West, IA	132	Jr.
Molly Wilson	Iowa City, West, IA	132	Jr.
Heidi Schmidt-Rundell	Iowa City, West, IA	182	Jr.
Kaitlyn Hansen	Iowa City, West, IA	120	Sr.
Manal Duah	Iowa City, West, IA	132	Sr.
Laurel Haverkamp	Iowa City, West, IA	138	Sr.
Mami Selemani	Iowa City, West, IA	152	Sr.
Salima Omari	Iowa City, West, IA	285	Sr.
Jordyn Waldrop	Iowa Valley, Marengo, IA	113	Fr.
Alexis Hoeppner	Iowa Valley, Marengo, IA	138	Fr.
Millie Peach	Iowa Valley, Marengo, IA	220	Jr.
Baylee McEntee	Keokuk, IA	195	So.
Faith Hatch	Knoxville, IA	138	Sr.
Kylie Hessenius	LeMars, IA	106	Fr.
Calla Langel	LeMars, IA	113	Fr.
Bailey Brady	LeMars, IA	126	Fr.
Maddie Keunen	LeMars, IA	126	Fr.
Isabella Manning	LeMars, IA	132	Fr.
Jacey Theisen	LeMars, IA	132	Fr.
Sidney Minar	LeMars, IA	138	So.
Juli Herrera	LeMars, IA	145	So.
Summer Gollhofer	LeMars, IA	106	Jr.
Jaycee Davison	LeMars, IA	126	Jr.
Josie Matgen	LeMars, IA	138	Jr.
Brooke Rood	LeMars, IA	195	Jr.
Jasmine Garcia	LeMars, IA	160	Sr.
Jecenta Sargisson	LeMars, IA	160	Sr.
Haley Kolker	LeMars, IA	182	Sr.
Brittney Brunssen	LeMars, IA	195	Sr.
Hannah Westra	LeMars, IA	220	Sr.
Ava McNeal	Lewis Central, IA	106	Fr.
Shaylee Sanders	Lewis Central, IA	113	Fr.

Anchal Chaudhari	Lewis Central, IA	132	Fr.
Sophie Barnes	Lewis Central, IA	138	Fr.
Dana Swebsky	Lewis Central, IA	145	Fr.
Taylor French	Lewis Central, IA	120	Sr.
Lauren Pulis	Linn-Mar, IA	120	Fr.
Jannell Avila	Lisbon, IA	132	Fr.
Catrina Sears	Logan-Magnolia, IA	120	Sr.
Olivia Diggins	Logan-Magnolia, IA	138	Sr.
Elizabeth Elliot	Lynnville-Sully, IA	106	Fr.
Hayleigh Dawson	Maquoketa, IA	138	Fr.
Jade Armbruster	Maquoketa, IA	113	Sr.
Anna Tuuri	Marion, IA	120	Fr.
Jordan Wheeler	Marion, IA	120	Fr.
Makenzie Goettsch	Marion, IA	126	Fr.
Morgan Hangartner	Marion, IA	152	Jr.
Kay Mundy	Marion, IA	145	Sr.
Josephine Wearmouth	Martensdale-St Marys, IA	132	So.
Kadence Pape	MFL MarMac, IA	120	Fr.
Isabella Bogdonovich	MFL MarMac, IA	106	So.
Marissa Cline	Mid-Prairie, IA	132	Fr.
Mia Garvey	Mid-Prairie, IA	138	Fr.
Rylee Vercande	Mid-Prairie, IA	126	So.
Madison Kelly	Mid-Prairie, IA	160	So.
Caitlyn Busch	Mid-Prairie, IA	145	Jr.
Sarah Meader	Mid-Prairie, IA	170	Jr.
Haley Bowman	Missouri Valley, IA	138	So.
Maddy Buffum	Missouri Valley, IA	160	Jr.
Icia Bouza	MOC-Floyd Valley, IA	113	Jr.
Amanda Gustafsson	MOC-Floyd Valley, IA	132	Jr.
Kristen Quiroz	MOC-Floyd Valley, IA	152	Sr.
Delia Rodriguez	MOC-Floyd Valley, IA	195	Sr.
Alaina Sunlin	Monticello, IA	106	Sr.
Abby Blint	Mount Pleasant, IA	106	So.
Tori Oelrich	Mount Vernon, IA	120	Fr.
Abby Morf	Mount Vernon, IA	138	Fr.
Maddy Plotz	Mount Vernon, IA	120	So.
Julia Wheeler	Mount Vernon, IA	126	Jr.
Reagan Light	Mount Vernon, IA	120	Sr.

Maddy Shultz	Mount Vernon, IA	170	Sr.
Virginia Cacho	Muscatine, IA	152	Jr.
Sam Henschen	MVAOCOU, IA	170	Sr.
Kyia Roths	Nashua-Plainfield, IA	126	Fr.
Toyia Griffin	Nashua-Plainfield, IA	152	Jr.
Camrae Schakel	Nevada, IA	152	Sr.
Addie Orth	New London, IA	106	So.
Patricia Baker	Newton, IA		Fr.
Kinzie Hardin	Newton, IA	106	Fr.
Raven Hoen	Newton, IA		So.
Emma Fox	Newton, IA	126	So.
Shyanne Valladores	Newton, IA	160	So.
Grace Brown	Newton, IA	285	Jr.
Bailey Cox	NH/TV, IA	138	Fr.
Tierney Perkins	NH/TV, IA	145	Fr.
Sophia Adams	NH/TV, IA	138	Jr.
Claire Quirk	NH/TV, IA	145	Jr.
Kylie Murray	North Cedar, Stanwood, IA	106	So.
Ashlynn Miller	North Cedar, Stanwood, IA	120	So.
Val Boleyn	North Fayette Valley, IA	170	Jr.
Abby Boehm	North Fayette Valley, IA	220	Jr.
Chole Grant	North Fayette Valley, IA	113	Sr.
Arianna Hill	North Mahaska, IA	120	Fr.
Libby Groom	North Mahaska, IA	126	Fr.
Avala Faber	North Scott, IA	106	Fr.
Bella Warm	North Scott, IA	113	Fr.
Greta Baker	North Scott, IA	132	Fr.
Jorie Hanenburg	North Scott, IA	160	Fr.
Abby Allen	North Scott, IA	182	Fr.
Chloe Strand	North Scott, IA	182	Fr.
Ava Garrard	North Scott, IA	132	So.
Maddie Gottschalk	North Scott, IA	138	So.
Meara Gottschalk	North Scott, IA	152	So.
Faith Rains	North Scott, IA	106	Jr.
Lily McDermott	North Scott, IA	113	Jr.
Glory Hansel	North Scott, IA	120	Jr.
Kyleigh Westlin	North Scott, IA	132	Jr.
Kara Rohlf	North Scott, IA	138	Jr.

McKenna Santee	North Scott, IA	138	Jr.
Caelan Long	North Scott, IA	152	Jr.
Maia Glover	North Scott, IA	132	Sr.
Olivia McDermott	North Scott, IA	132	Sr.
Alexis Cary	North Scott, IA	138	Sr.
Jesse Taflinger	North Scott, IA	195	Sr.
Misheelt Tumurbaatar	North Tama, IA	132	Sr.
Juana Jones	Notre Dame, Burlington, IA	145	So.
Lauren Hamilton	Oelwein, IA	120	So.
Isabella Reinhart	Oelwein, IA	126	So.
Morgan Alber	Oelwein, IA	138	So.
Naomi Gaede	Oelwein, IA	145	Jr.
Kennedy Lape	Oelwein, IA	152	Jr.
Abbie Dahl	Oelwein, IA	170	Jr.
Kilynn Harbst	Okoboji/HMS, IA	145	Fr.
Kiera McCoy	Okoboji/HMS, IA	113	So.
Elli Hanson	Okoboji/HMS, IA	126	So.
Trista Tanner	Okoboji/HMS, IA	170	So.
Haley Dodge	Okoboji/HMS, IA	220	So.
Sarae Sehman	Okoboji/HMS, IA	113	Jr.
Kylan Green	Okoboji/HMS, IA	152	Jr.
Jalynn Goodale	Osage, IA	113	Fr.
Azure Christensen	Osage, IA	126	Fr.
Katelyn Johnston	Osage, IA	126	Fr.
Sydney Muller	Osage, IA	132	Fr.
Leah Grimm	Osage, IA	170	Fr.
Mary Ann Fox	Osage, IA	145	So.
Karlie Wagner	Osage, IA	113	Jr.
Emma Grimm	Osage, IA	126	Jr.
Katerina Smith	Osage, IA	126	Jr.
Ainsley Dodd	Osage, IA	138	Jr.
Brynley Schouweiler	Osage, IA	138	Jr.
Grace Mallory	Osage, IA	170	Jr.
Abigail Cockrum	Osage, IA	285	Jr.
Madison Adams	Osage, IA	113	Sr.
Clarissa Huisman	Osage, IA	132	Sr.
Makayla Mostek	Osage, IA	145	Sr.
Melanie Bye	Osage, IA	160	Sr.

Raeann Elliot	Oskaloosa, IA	126	Fr.
Emma Strayer	Ottumwa, IA	120	Fr.
Jade Davis	Ottumwa, IA		Jr.
Sabrina Morrow	Ottumwa, IA		Sr.
Jaime Thorpe	Panorama, IA	106	Sr.
Hayleigh Spray	PCM, Monroe, IA	126	So.
Ruth Gorman	PCM, Monroe, IA	152	So.
Viola Humpal	PCM, Monroe, IA	220	So.
Margo Chipps	PCM, Monroe, IA	106	Jr.
Jaden Eighmey	PCM, Monroe, IA	132	Jr.
Hannah Birkenholtz	PCM, Monroe, IA	220	Jr.
Hailey Peterson	Perry, IA	106	Fr.
Taylor Atwell	Perry, IA	113	Fr.
Martha Turrado	Perry, IA	126	Fr.
Desi Drieling	Pleasant Valley, IA	120	Fr.
Desirea Drieling	Pleasant Valley, IA	120	Fr.
Chloe Clemons	Pleasant Valley, IA	120	Sr.
Brynn Miller	Pleasantville, IA	138	So.
Sayde Mull	Pleasantville, IA	113	Sr.
Khiaya Burns	Postville, IA	113	Jr.
Julissa Elsbernd	Postville, IA		Sr.
Kim Meyer	Ridge View, IA	113	Fr.
Audrey Kalin	Ridge View, IA	170	So.
Karen Meyer	Ridge View, IA	195	So.
Alexis Turnquist	Ridge View, IA	195	Jr.
Iliana Yanes	Riverside, Oakland, IA	285	Jr.
Sam Hendrian	Roland-Story, IA	160	Fr.
Morgan Griffin	Sioux Central, IA	170	So.
Michelle Anderson	Sioux Central, IA	120	Jr.
Angeleena Rasmussen	Sioux City East, IA	113	Fr.
Yareli Morales	Sioux City East, IA	120	So.
Melissa Weagbah	Sioux City North, IA	160	Fr.
Karina Esquivel	Sioux City North, IA	120	Sr.
Christina Ly	Sioux City North, IA	120	Sr.
Jennifer Morales	Sioux City West, IA	160	So.
NeVaeh Pettiford	Sioux City West, IA	160	So.
Jazmine Murdock	Sioux City West, IA	132	Jr.
Addison Burden	Solon, IA	138	Fr.

Cheyenne Mulford	Solon, IA	120	So.
Summer Rajotte	South Central Calhoun, IA	126	Fr.
Delanie Westcott	South Central Calhoun, IA	132	Fr.
Hannah Payne	South Central Calhoun, IA	126	Sr.
Morgan Woosley	South Tama County, IA	152	Jr.
Ashlee Sanders	Southeast Polk, IA	145	So.
Angie Clark	Southeast Warren/ Melcher-Dallas, IA	182	Fr.
Lynzie Drake	Southeast Warren/ Melcher-Dallas, IA	126	So.
Riley Spencer	Southwest Iowa, IA	113	Fr.
Kennedy Lamkins	Southwest Iowa, IA	145	Jr.
Adyson Lundquist	Southwest Valley, IA	113	Fr.
Aliyah Schon	Spencer, IA	126	Fr.
Krystol Luna Rosales	Spencer, IA	120	So.
Emma Strohman	Spencer, IA	138	So.
Erin Strohman	Spencer, IA	182	So.
Lillia Williams	St. Albert, IA	132	So.
Elly Berry	St. Edmond, IA	132	So.
Kari German	Starmont, IA	113	Sr.
Grace Jones	Sumner-Fredericksburg, IA	120	So.
Raina Shonka	Sumner-Fredericksburg, IA	132	Jr.
Kylee Jordan	Sumner-Fredericksburg, IA	120	Sr.
Isabelle Meyer	Sumner-Fredericksburg, IA	126	Sr.
Katelyn Bartels	Sumner-Fredericksburg, IA	138	Sr.
Alexis Franco	Sumner-Fredericksburg, IA	152	Sr.
Elizabeth Fox	Sumner-Fredericksburg, IA	170	Sr.
Elise Mowatt	Tripoli, IA	138	Jr.
Olivia Smith	Union, LaPorte City, IA	113	Fr.
Sarah Michael	Union, LaPorte City, IA	106	So.
Jazmyn Knutson	Valley, West Des Moines, IA	132	So.
Saida Komjo	Valley, West Des Moines, IA	138	Jr.
Laura Kipusu	Valley, West Des Moines, IA	145	Jr.
Chloe Curtis	Van Buren County, IA	138	Jr.
Bailey Weeks	Vinton-Shellsburg, IA	160	So.
Alia Gale	Vinton-Shellsburg, IA	160	Jr.
Lillie Lamont	Vinton-Shellsburg, IA	126	Sr.
Amelia Birker	Vinton-Shellsburg, IA	152	Sr.

Avery Waterhouse	WACO, Wayland, IA	120	Fr.
Marley McSwain	Wahlert, Dubuque, IA	182	Fr.
Mia Kunnert	Wahlert, Dubuque, IA	132	So.
Ellie Meyer	Wahlert, Dubuque, IA	132	So.
Alaina Duggan	Wahlert, Dubuque, IA	138	So.
Alix Oliver	Wahlert, Dubuque, IA	113	Jr.
Brenna Schultz	Wahlert, Dubuque, IA	113	Jr.
Bree Buxton	Wahlert, Dubuque, IA	120	Jr.
Ariana Yaklich	Wahlert, Dubuque, IA	120	Jr.
Ivy Dearstone	Wahlert, Dubuque, IA	132	Jr.
Hayley Welbes	Wahlert, Dubuque, IA	145	Jr.
Anna Kalb	Wahlert, Dubuque, IA	160	Jr.
Grace Burke	Wahlert, Dubuque, IA	120	Sr.
Jayden Bartow	Wahlert, Dubuque, IA	126	Sr.
Ellie Timmerman	Wahlert, Dubuque, IA	126	Sr.
Rachel Eddy	Wahlert, Dubuque, IA	132	Sr.
Maria Kircher	Wahlert, Dubuque, IA	138	Sr.
Aliyah Carter	Wahlert, Dubuque, IA	152	Sr.
Maggie Friederick	Wahlert, Dubuque, IA	152	Sr.
Alaina Schmidt	Wahlert, Dubuque, IA	152	Sr.
Karlie Welbes	Wahlert, Dubuque, IA	152	Sr.
Julia Norton	Wahlert, Dubuque, IA	160	Sr.
Paige Hummel	Wahlert, Dubuque, IA	170	Sr.
Teegan Sulentich	Washington, IA	170	Fr.
Jayden Bentley	Waterloo East, IA	170	Jr.
Victoria Knight	Waterloo West, IA	106	Jr.
Sydney Burt	Waterloo West, IA	132	Sr.
Alli Schaffer	Waterloo West, IA	170	Sr.
Lindsey Bass	Waterloo West, IA	285	Sr.
Rylee Rodish	Waukee, IA	113	So.
Jordyn Nikkel	Waukee, IA	126	So.
Stephanie Badtram	Waukee, IA	113	Jr.
Sydney Clevenger	Waukee, IA	160	Jr.
Madi Nagra	Waukee, IA	195	Sr.
Katherine Ogden	Waukee, IA	195	Sr.
Meridian Snitker	Waukon, IA	126	So.
Peyton Verthein	Waukon, IA	160	So.
Regan Griffith	Waukon, IA	126	Jr.

Rylee Yant	Waverly-Shell Rock, IA	106	Fr.
Kyla Foy	Waverly-Shell Rock, IA	120	Fr.
Brinley Meier	Waverly-Shell Rock, IA	120	Fr.
Miranda Janssen	Waverly-Shell Rock, IA	145	Fr.
Nicole Miller-Cummings	Waverly-Shell Rock, IA	152	Fr.
Haidyn Snyder	Waverly-Shell Rock, IA	160	Fr.
Zoe Blanchette	Waverly-Shell Rock, IA	126	So.
Annika Behrends	Waverly-Shell Rock, IA	132	So.
Kailey Hervol	Waverly-Shell Rock, IA	132	So.
Macy Smith	Waverly-Shell Rock, IA	132	So.
Avery Meier	Waverly-Shell Rock, IA	126	Jr.
Maria Cooper	Waverly-Shell Rock, IA	132	Jr.
Kaelei Tellinghuisen	Waverly-Shell Rock, IA	132	Jr.
Marley Hagarty	Waverly-Shell Rock, IA	138	Jr.
Mattie Janssen	Waverly-Shell Rock, IA	138	Jr.
Gayle Robinson	Waverly-Shell Rock, IA	170	Jr.
Ryleigh Rinnels	Waverly-Shell Rock, IA	182	Jr.
Jenn Peters	Waverly-Shell Rock, IA		Sr.
Olivia Sowle	Waverly-Shell Rock, IA	113	Sr.
Cailey Reyna	Waverly-Shell Rock, IA	132	Sr.
Kennedy Eastman	Waverly-Shell Rock, IA	152	Sr.
Katy Kellum	Waverly-Shell Rock, IA	152	Sr.
Bailey Walsh	Waverly-Shell Rock, IA	170	Sr.
Payton Hitt	Wayne, Corydon, IA	113	Fr.
Sarah Moorman	Wayne, Corydon, IA	132	Sr.
Lily Flint	West Harrison, Mondamin, IA	126	Jr.
Magaly Kivi	West Liberty, IA	120	Fr.
Mylei Henderson	West Liberty, IA	152	So.
Isabel Morrison	West Liberty, IA	160	So.
Alexis Partida	West Liberty, IA	113	Sr.
Annemarie Eriksen	West Liberty, IA	138	Sr.
Summer Allen	West Lyon, IA	106	Jr.
Cady Perez	Westwood, Sloan, IA	106	Sr.
Kaity Anderson	Westwood, Sloan, IA	138	Sr.
Sierra Hinrickson	Westwood, Sloan, IA	145	Sr.
Braxton Dewald.	Westwood, Sloan, IA	220	Sr.
Janessa Ervin	Wilton, IA	106	Fr.
Mea Burkle	Wilton, IA	132	Jr.

Sierra Brammer	Woodbine, IA	132	Fr.
Audrey Ireland	Woodbine, IA	113	Jr.
Kaitlyn Guy	Woodbine, IA	126	Sr.
Charity Mickles	Woodward-Granger, IA	113	Fr.

The Authors

Diane Fannon-Langton, retired after more than 40 years at The Gazette in Cedar Rapids, continues to write a weekly area history column, "The Time Machine," for the paper. She has authored two books based on the column. Her first loves, however, are her husband, Richard, their children and grandchildren.

Tricia Andersen lives in Iowa with her husband, Brian and her three children – her sons, Jake and Jon, and her daughter, Alex. She graduated from the University of Iowa with a Bachelor of Arts in English and from Kirkwood Community College with an Associate of Arts degree in Communications Media/Public Relations.
Along with writing (which she loves to do), Tricia practices Brazilian Jiu Jitsu, coaches and participates in track and field, reads, sews and is involved in many of her children's activities.